REA

A Ragged Mountain Press
WOMAN'S GUIDE

❄ WINTER SPORTS

A Ragged Mountain Press
WOMAN'S GUIDE

❄ WINTER SPORTS

ISEULT DEVLIN

Series Editor, Molly Mulhern Gross

RAGGED MOUNTAIN PRESS / McGRAW-HILL

Camden, Maine • New York • San Francisco • Washington, D.C. • Auckland
Bogotá • Caracas • Lisbon • London • Madrid • Mexico City • Milan
Montreal • New Delhi • San Juan • Singapore • Sydney • Tokyo • Toronto

• •

"**E**very time it snowed, I felt like something exciting was going to happen—
it was just like magic."

—Cecile Johnson, age 85, artist

• •

Look for these other Ragged Mountain Press Woman's Guides

Backpacking, Adrienne Hall

Canoeing, Laurie Gullion

Climbing, Shelley Presson

Fly-Fishing, Dana Rikimaru

Golf, Susan Comolli

Mountaineering, Andrea Gabbard

Powerboating, Sandy Lindsey

Sailing, Doris Colgate

Scuba Diving, Claire Walter

Sea Kayaking, Shelley Johnson

Skiing, Maggie Loring

Snowboarding, Julia Carlson

• •

Ragged Mountain Press
A Division of The McGraw-Hill Companies

10 9 8 7 6 5 4 3 2 1

Copyright © 2001 Iseult Devlin

Foreword copyright © 2001 Molly Mulhern Gross

Library of Congress Cataloging-in-Publication Data

Devlin, Iseult.

    Winter sports / Iseult Devlin.

        p.   cm.—(A Ragged Mountain Press woman's guide)

    Includes bibliographical references (p.) and index.

    ISBN 0-07-158188-X (alk. paper)

    1. Winter sports. 2. Sports for women. I. Title.

        II. Series

GV841.C48 2000

796.9—dc21   00-042536

Questions regarding the content of this book should be addressed to
Ragged Mountain Press
P.O. Box 220
Camden, ME 04843
http://www.raggedmountainpress.com

Questions regarding the ordering of this book should be addressed to
The McGraw-Hill Companies
Customer Service Department
P.O. Box 547
Blacklick, OH 43004
Retail customers: 1-800-262-4729
Bookstores: 1-800-722-4726

This book is printed on 70# Citation.

Printed by Quebecor Printing Company, Fairfield, PA

Design by Carol Inouye, Inkstone Communications Design

Production management by Janet Robbins

Page layout by Shannon Thomas

Edited by Alice Bennett

Illustrations by Elayne Sears.

All photographs by Dennis Curran/Sports File except for the following: page 13 courtesy Helen Olsson; page 17 (top), 51, 52 courtesy Cheyenne Rouse; page 17 (bottom), 95 courtesy Patrick Pachod; page 18, 80 (bottom), 91, 96 (top) courtesy Okemo Mountain Resort; pages 25, 26 courtesy Tubbs Snowshoe Company; page 27 courtesy PhotoDisc; page 29, 43 (top) courtesy Cold As Ice; page 39, 125 courtesy Obermeyer; pages 40 (top), 43 (bottom), 46 courtesy North Face; pages 40 (bottom), 42 courtesy Lowe Alpine; page 45 courtesy Bolle; page 47 courtesy Teton Toppers; page 48 courtesy Leedom; page 62 courtesy Atlas Snowshoes; page 64 courtesy Todd Powell/ Outside Images; page 67 courtesy Rick Lovett; page 70 (top) courtesy Rossignol; page 70 (middle) courtesy Paul Petersen; page 79 courtesy Alpina Sports; page 80 (top) courtesy Tecnica/Volkl/Obermeyer, Biege Jones; page 114 courtesy Sharon Wissel; page 115 courtesy University of Maine.

• •

DEDICATION

To my mother, Deirdre, for turning me on to winter and inspiring me to learn to ski. To my dad, John, for motivating me to participate in sports and talking tech. And, to my husband, Geoff, for being my winter sports buddy who is always game for any adventure.

• •

Foreword ❄

I hate the cold," my neighbor remarked at a recent gathering, her response to my gushing about glorious snow conditions. At first I wondered why she would turn her back on winter, the most rewarding and challenging season. Then I remembered the few times I'd been wet and cold—caught by a sudden winter rain or out in cotton socks that sucked the warmth out of my feet. Cold, wet feet are the worst: they induce a full body chill, sending even the hardiest of souls indoors, fast. But I can count on one hand the number of times I've had uncomfortable winter experiences. Learning how to stay warm when the mercury drops below freezing and the wind begins to roar—and, ironically, how to keep from getting overheated, see pages 42–44—is key to enjoying this undiscovered season.

Getting comfortable outdoors in the cold is well worth it, for winter is truly an outdoorswoman's paradise. Few activities restore one's soul more effectively than a ski across freshly fallen snow in a towering pine forest. The woods are so quiet your own breathing seems disruptive. My neighbor hasn't gazed in wonder from the top of a winter mountain, where the world lies at your feet, miles of open, snow-covered terrain beckoning for a graceful traverse on snowboard or a leisurely amble on snowshoes. Nor has my friend ever felt the delight in starting off across the obsidian-smooth surface of a frozen northern pond, free to carve her own route across the ice, away from the crowds of skating rinks.

Winter Sports: A Woman's Guide is for women who haven't yet discovered the joy of winter. It's also for women who unwittingly ventured out skiing with cotton socks or with ice skates that failed to support their ankles, women who endured miserable first times and are wondering just how others can find joy and pleasure outdoors in winter. This guide is written from a woman's perspective, with a calm and straightforward approach to the questions you have about staying warm, approaching the rental staff at the ski lodge, or learning how to tell if the local pond ice is thick enough for a skate.

What's so different about the way women learn? If you're like me, you like to hear a description or overview of a move or tactic before launching into it. I guess you could say I'm a fan of the talk-it-over-and-think-it-through-first school of learning. It gives me a chance to ask questions *before* I'm asked to strap on my snowshoes or rent my first pair of skis. I also like to hear advice from someone who is like me, someone I know and trust. And I like to learn in a group so I can hear other folks' questions—and know I'm not the only one wondering which ski goes on which foot (see page 71)!

We've done our best to mimic these learning conditions in The Ragged Mountain Press Woman's Guides. Here you'll find lots of women's voices: your instructor's, of course, but also voices of women from all walks of life who have learned these outdoor activities. *Winter Sports: A Woman's Guide* provides solutions, advice, and stories from women who have done what you are about to do: explore the world of winter sports. I hope Iseult's words and approach help get you out to explore and enjoy, by yourself or with a friend. I'll look for you out there.

When you get a break from playing in the snow, drop us a note to tell us how we're doing and how we can improve these guides to best suit you and your learning style.

MOLLY MULHERN GROSS
Series Editor, The Ragged Mountain Press Woman's Guides
Camden, Maine
September 2000

*An avid outdoorswoman, Molly Mulhern Gross enjoys running,
hiking, camping, sea kayaking, telemark skiing, in-line skating,
biking, and snowboarding. She is Director of Editing, Design,
and Production at Ragged Mountain Press and International Marine.*

CONTENTS ❄

❄ CONTENTS

Acknowledgments ❄

Of course, I'd like to thank everyone at Ragged Mountain Press for making this book happen, especially Molly Mulhern Gross for inspiring the series and for having the patience to offer helpful advice along the way. Also thanks to Pam Cruickshank of Okemo Mountain Resort for lending extra support in getting our photo shoot done on a late spring day. I really appreciated the snowmobile rides up and down the mountain, both for their efficiency as well as for keeping me and my high-risk pregnancy (now little Ronan) safe.

This book would not have been possible without my ski team cohorts such as Gregg, Leif, Paul, and especially George, who had faith in my abilities to persevere and to become an excellent skier, although at the time I was a mess on the slopes. Thanks to my best friend, Kathy, who was with me from the start and on all those fun high-school trips to Hunter. I'd like to thank my sister, Ann, who turned me onto skiing without lifts—we would just hike up on our skis (alpine touring) and find our own virgin powder in the Alps. Thanks also to John Henry Auran, who was responsible for getting my foot in the door at *Skiing* magazine, which led to my career in the industry, and to Rick Kahl, who gave me tons of opportunities to write at *Skiing Trade News* (even on the weekends!).

There are others to thank, I'm sure. During all my years working in the industry, I've met countless women who have taken me into the backcountry, given me tips on how to be a better cross-country skier, and simply inspired me by being incredible athletes in winter.

❄ Introduction: Why I Love Winter

This is a book for two kinds of people: winter lovers and winter haters. Winter haters should know that you don't have to hibernate—there are many ways to get active outside in the winter. I know many people who dread the cold—my dad, for one—yet I think taking part in winter activities could make anyone look forward to the season or at least make it more tolerable. In this book those who already love the cold will find out just how much there is to do during wintertime.

My main cold-weather sport has been skiing, but before I ever skied I loved to ice-skate and go sledding. Since I started skiing when I was 13, I've been introduced to so many other winter sports—cross-country skiing, snowboarding, backcountry skiing, heli-skiing—that there never seems to be enough time, or enough snow, to try it all. It's been my mission to pass along my love and enthusiasm for winter sports as much as I can. The people I take out to try skiing or snowboarding—no matter how difficult they may find it—all wear big smiles at the end of the day and have newfound energy and enthusiasm.

And I like to introduce people to winter sports. Not just because I once taught skiing, but because I truly believe skiing changed my life. I first started skiing with my best friend, Kathy, because somehow it seemed important to go with a buddy. We immediately became hooked and skied a few weekends a year. When I went to college I joined the ski club, and by my sophomore year I decided I was ready for the ski team. At this point my skiing was really not very good—I had maybe twenty total ski days under my belt. It showed: I barely made the Rutgers University Ski Team, which took fifteen men but only five women, and I was probably the worst person on the team. But I persevered. When it was icy and one of the top female skiers was too scared to ski on the bulletproof ice, I wasn't picky. I didn't know any better, so I raced down the ice—fearless. That helped me move up the ranks quickly.

During my junior year I went to France to study, choosing a location close to the mountains so I could ski a lot. I joined the ski club at Université de Grenoble and competed in races throughout the winter. Even though my peers were a bunch of 14-year-olds, I improved a lot, and by the time I returned

Author Iseult Devlin takes a breather while hiking up to Tuckerman's Ravine, the "extreme skiing" mecca of the East.

to Rutgers I was the best woman on the team and always finished in the top three for the entire collegiate league. And I was better than most of the guys. That experience did worlds for my confidence and gave me a whole new outlook.

With perseverance and hard work, I became better at the sport than I ever dreamed of. And to help more women get involved, I started a ski team at Douglass College (at the time, a women's college within Rutgers University) that was all women. We raced with the guys and were on the same basic team, but with the funds from Douglass College we were able to expand from five women to fifteen. And having a separate team meant the women got better start times at the races, so we didn't always go last and ski rutted-up courses. I saw that with a little effort I could make a big difference and influence many women who raced with me as well as others later on.

After college I went back to Europe to travel, to learn languages, and (of course) to ski. I was lucky enough to land a job as a ski instructor at the famous Kitzbühel ski resort in Austria. Now I was actually making money while enjoying the sport I loved. Because I was a woman, I had to start out teaching children. I didn't like that much, not because I don't like kids, but because I was stuck with the ones who were really too young to ski, so it was more like babysitting than teaching. After a couple of weeks, though, they ran out of male instructors and moved me to the adult school. I enjoyed teaching so much that I stayed for a second season—something I hadn't planned on. Skiing in Europe was a world apart from New Jersey and New England—the mountains were so beautiful and the weather usually so sunny that deciding to stay was easy.

Since then I've remained deeply involved in the ski world, and over the years I've learned the joys of other winter sports. Winter is never long enough, and when I travel to the mountains I never know what to bring: snowboard, cross-country skis, downhill skis, or snowshoes? I try to do it all.

Even my career has turned out to be winter oriented. I worked at *Skiing* magazine and *Skiing Trade News* for twelve years. For eight years I was editor-in-chief of *Skiing Trade News*. During that time I traveled all over the world and learned just about everything there is to know about the ski industry.

I've also had the opportunity to introduce a lot of people to winter sports. I taught my mother, Deirdre, how to cross-country ski when she was in her late 50s, and when she turned 60 I persuaded her to try downhill skiing. I truly believe you're never too old! I turned my sister-in-law, Molly, on to skiing and have taught both my nephews, Declan and Rory, to alpine and cross-country ski. Though I haven't yet taken my own little one skiing (he's only six months old), I know what it means to "take the family skiing." It takes a lot of organization, patience, and attention to safety.

I enjoyed teaching my mother and nephews to ski as much as I enjoyed putting my skins (adhesive strips that allow skis to grab the snow for walking uphill) on skis to do the Haute

Route—a five-day trek across glaciers and high passes in the Alps. You stay in mountain huts and don't get to shower for days. It sounds disgusting, but I felt on top of the world afterward. It was the best trip of my life for building my confidence and making me feel renewed. This is the type of experience more women should try. This book can show you how to get started, whether it's something as adventurous as the Haute Route or as simple as a Sunday stroll through the park on snowshoes. It's all fun!

I meet a lot of women who once enjoyed being outdoors in the winter but for some reason stopped. Some had a bad experience skiing or snowboarding—perhaps the wrong instructor. Or they tried the sport on a freezing day when even the most die-hard enthusiasts wouldn't venture out. They like to talk about the experience and sound as if they'd like to give it another try. But either they don't know how to get started or they think they're too old or out of shape.

In this book I hope to inspire those women and others to give winter sports a try. You'll find stories of women who persevered to overcome all sorts of obstacles, ending up as enthusiastic participants. You'll find information on special clinics and instruction weeks for women. And you'll learn about women's equipment and how it can help you in the sports you want to pursue. Read on and learn how you can make this the year you get back out in the cold.

Chapter 1

❄ BEING ACTIVE

This is it. This is the year you're going to try skiing or snowboarding or even snowshoeing. Maybe you've tried downhill skiing or cross-country skiing sometime in the past, but for one reason or another you stopped going out to play in the snow.

Perhaps you played outside in winter when you were a child. It was easy then: Mom and Dad organized everything, and your job was to have fun building igloos or ice-skating at the local rink. When you got too cold, your parents or someone else had a warm fire and hot chocolate waiting.

It was so much fun. Cold, brisk air—even a howling wind—made you feel alive and gave you naturally rosy cheeks. It was invigorating, and you felt empowered by battling the elements.

Getting outside in the winter is peaceful and exhilarating —especially in a beautiful area like the French Alps, a popular **downhill skiing** destination.

But somehow things changed. Do we grow up or maybe just grow boring? Or is it just the natural passage into the three Rs: responsibility, responsibility, responsibility?

Who said **snowboarding** is intimidating? Two new snowboarders relax while listening to tips from a pro.

• •

"**E**very time it snowed, I felt like something exciting was going to happen—it was just like magic."

—Cecile Johnson, age 85, artist

• •

Maybe, as you say, you just hate the cold. So you act like a bear and hibernate. How often have you thought about getting active in winter, then chickened out? It's too cold, it's too much of a hassle, you don't know how to get started: it's easy to come up with a reason not to go out. Whatever the rationale, you're not alone— women who quit winter sports or never try them in the first place have a long list of reasons. These are the top ten alibis for avoiding winter activities.

- **I don't have time.** It's really a question of making the time. Being active in winter is much healthier than shopping the malls, organizing the house, or just hanging out. It's worth the effort, and it won't be long before you'll feel comfortable with winter sports. In less than an hour you can learn the basics of ice-skating, cross-country skiing, or snowshoeing. Skiing and snowboarding take a bit longer, but after a day of lessons you can be making turns and coming down the hill.

- **I don't like cold weather.** Winter doesn't have to mean feeling cold if you wear the right clothes. You may already own the basic things you'll need—long underwear, a fleece top, a waterproof shell or a jacket, a hat and gloves. If you have to buy some pieces, they can also be used just for going around town or walking the dog—you'll be much warmer and dryer with clothing designed to protect you. (See chapter 3 for details on what to wear.)

Cross-country skiing, like other aerobic sports, can generate the body heat necessary to keep you quite warm in most weather.

- **It takes too long to learn to ski or snowboard.** Some people need longer than others, but a good instructor will take things one step at a time, starting you off on a flat area. Next you'll go to a gentle incline and try to make one turn. Before you know it, you'll be linking two or three turns and skiing or snowboarding down the hill. (Refer to the individual chapters for tips on how to get started in each of the winter sports in this book.)

- **I have a family to take care of.** Bring them along. These sports are fun for families. Ski and snowboard areas have all sorts of special deals for kids. At most resorts, children six and under ride the lifts for free.

- **I'm not a good enough athlete.** You don't have to be particularly athletic or coordinated to try winter sports. Women of all fitness levels and abilities have succeeded. Sliding on snow or ice does take some getting used to, but once you get comfortable with the movement, you'll find that learning is just a simple progression of steps. (For tips on getting into shape for winter sports, see chapter 2, pages 35–37.)

- **I'm too nervous.** It's always nerve-racking to try something new, but once you do you'll feel as if you can do anything. Riding a chairlift, sliding on snow, or skating across the ice is more daring than the average sport. But pushing yourself to do something adventurous makes you feel stronger. (You'll learn about riding a chairlift, ice-skating, and more in the following chapters.)

- **I'm too old to learn—winter sports are for kids.** You're never too old to try! Many people learn to ski or snowboard or cross-country ski or ice-skate in their thirties, forties, or fifties. Some even try in their sixties or seventies. It may be easier for kids, but that's mainly because they have less fear, not because they're better coordinated or more athletic. (Read about how other women got into winter sports later in this chapter.)

Ice-skating is probably the least expensive winter sport to buy into, since it requires only skates.

- **I'm afraid.** It's normal to be afraid to try something new and adventurous. Talk about your fears with an instructor. He or she can make all the difference in getting you started the right way. If need be, snowboard instructors will even ride backward holding your hands while you learn to make turns. Ski instructors can do the same thing.

- **I'll get hurt.** You can get hurt doing anything—even walking down the street. If you learn these sports in a controlled manner, it's easy to avoid injury. If you're really nervous, choose a day when conditions are optimal, with soft snow and sunny skies.

- **It's too expensive.** Some aspects of these sports are expensive, but there are ways to save. Some suggestions: check out smaller resorts, go at midweek, join a club, borrow clothing. I'll address inexpensive purchasing options in the following chapters.

WINTER SPORTS ARE EASIER THAN EVER

One wonderful thing about going out in the snow now is that winter apparel is so much better than when I was growing up. Winter clothing isn't as bulky. It's lightweight and easy to move around in. Materials have improved, making it easy to stay warm and cozy without feeling like a blimp. (Chapter 3 includes details on how to choose winter clothing.)

This is a great time to learn the most popular winter sports. The equipment in each of the sports covered in this book has improved a lot. In skiing, for example, breakthroughs in equipment design and materials have made it easier to learn and to progress quickly. Snowboarding, too, has easy-to-turn beginner boards and boards that take a woman's physique into consideration. Snowshoes no longer look like giant tennis rackets. They're lightweight and grip better than the wooden snowshoes of the past. Even cross-country gear has changed. Shorter skis make it easier to start Nordic skiing. (For more information on equipment, refer to the chapters on different winter sports.)

Perhaps you aren't active in winter because you're a dropout and you think it's too late to go back, for all those same reasons: I'm too old, I'm out of shape, I don't have time, and so on. Or you think you'll have to learn all over again. You won't. Skiing, ice-skating, and snowboarding are skills that never leave you. As with riding a bicycle, once you learn you don't forget the moves.

Most people who have dropped out of downhill skiing, cross-country skiing, or snowboarding and try those sports again will find things much easier than before. The new, shaped alpine skis make it easier to turn. More flexible snowboards are easier to maneuver, and new cross-country ski designs make it easier to glide along.

The slopes themselves are better manicured. Even if it hasn't snowed for weeks, man-made snow plus a resort's meticulous grooming make the surface easy to ski or snowboard on. Lift lines? They rarely exist anymore. It's not like the old days when you'd wait in line most of the day to get five or six runs down the mountain. Now, with fewer lines and high-speed lifts, you can get five or six runs in a couple of hours. In fact a half day of skiing or snowboarding is plenty, and you can save money by buying a half-day lift ticket.

Maybe you've tried downhill or cross-country skiing once or twice. Perhaps you went with a boyfriend or husband. One woman I know went to Stowe, Vermont, on her honeymoon and has only bad memories. When I told her I skied a lot, she immediately had to tell me, "I hate winter and cold weather." When she described the honeymoon and what an awful time she had, it became clear why she hated winter and everything associated with it. She tried skiing with the wrong equipment on an icy slope that was too difficult for a beginner—her husband's idea. That first exposure was bad enough to make it her last. It always frustrates me to meet some-

Beautifully groomed slopes make it easy for both **snowboarders** and **downhill skiers** to enjoy the mountain.

one who has had an unhappy experience because it's so easy to make the first time a positive adventure. For starters, I advise not letting your significant other teach you unless he has been a professional instructor or is truly an expert.

In general, women approach sports differently than men do. For example, I like to know what to expect before I just go out and do something—to come up with a plan of action before I plunge down a slope. My husband is different. He jumps right in with little regard for what the conditions might be like or what danger lurks ahead. He's convinced he can just power his way through any situation he encounters. I'm confident I could do the same, but I prefer to avoid risks. Why not find out about them first rather than later? Many guys have told me tales of being taken to the top of the mountain as first-timers by their "friends." Most made it down in one piece, but they wouldn't choose that method of "learning" again.

Men also don't learn the same way women do. I was with a couple who were cross-country skiing for the first time. She wanted to take the lessons, but when he found out it would be an extra $20 he said, "Why bother? We can do it on our own." I've seen plenty of guys trying to teach their female companions or kids by shouting something obvious like "Turn!" If it were that easy, who'd need a teacher in the first place? It's best to go with an objective pro who can show you the ropes the right way.

HOW AND WHY THEY GOT STARTED

Women are attracted to winter sports for various reasons. For some, taking them up has led to their becoming year-round athletes or starting new careers. Here are some of my favorite stories from women who changed their lives through sports and who overcame challenges of their own to get started.

Lisa Winston

Lisa, who owns Peak Exposure, a public-relations firm based in Boulder, Colorado, got into outdoor sports while working on sports-related accounts at an agency. Although she had skied in the past, at the time she didn't take part in any of the activities she was writing about.

Her memories of downhill skiing were bad ones. "My very first downhill ski experience was back East. I was 16 years old. I took the rope tow to the top of Blumont ski area. I went up, turned around, and came down. I had no lessons—it was sheer fright. I didn't even know you were supposed to turn—I thought it was like a ski jump. I took my skis off and never went back."

She dabbled in cross-country skiing when she was in her twenties, but again, she never had a proper lesson and always ended up on the wrong terrain and often on bad snow—glare ice conditions. Then a few years ago a client offered to pay for a semiprivate ski lesson.

"The real thrill, and what continues to motivate me to ski, is the view and the scenery and how absolutely gorgeous it can be, even while riding the chairlift. I watch people who ski well and say, 'OK, I want to do that.' For me, skiing is not a social event. It's a very solitary issue—it's me against the snow conditions and the little personal triumphs I make along the way. It's a triumph just to get down the slopes when you get into terrain over your head. I also learned quickly after a few lessons to read the terrain as you're going up the lift and plan which slope you want to go down."

Today Lisa is not as fanatical as some, but she goes out five to ten days a year, depending on the weather. And skiing has led to other triumphs. She climbed Kilimanjaro, the highest mountain in Africa. And she now takes part in many other sports. In the winter she likes to go out on her snowshoes, whether it's up some of the hills in Boulder or to one of the many high mountain passes nearby. Before Lisa started skiing, she wasn't particularly athletic. Now she's quite the athlete, tackling black diamond runs on the slopes, running in the summer, and planning more endurance trips like Kilimanjaro.

> "What I love about skiing is you're absolutely in touch with nature. That feeling you have after skiing. The cold isn't cold anymore. Winter isn't bad anymore. I love the feeling of being totally relaxed and satisfied, feeling clean and fresh."
>
> —Gertie Kanzler

Gertie Kanzler

When German native Gertie accompanied her husband on ski trips in the early 1980s, she didn't even think about skiing herself. "I thought it was too late. I remember sitting in the lodge at Okemo watching people skiing down—it was so fascinating. But I thought, 'Not in a lifetime would I be able to do that.' I wanted to be able to, though. So I'd sit all day in the lodge staring up at the mountain, smoking cigarettes, bored to death." One day Gertie got fed up and decided she was never going to sit in a lodge again. She put on her husband's old ski pants and jacket and went with him to a small mountain in Pennsylvania. "I was scared. I was hanging on the rope tow—it was the only thing they had. I fell off that thing soon enough." Gertie's biggest fear was that the mountain would pull her straight down. "I had nightmares about standing at the top of the mountain and just shooting down. I didn't know you could control your speed and go slowly—going from side to side." After that first experience Gertie felt OK, and she went to another small ski area in Pennsylvania.

"What happened is, all of a sudden I started to love nature, and I didn't think it was just about freezing. That ski experience changed me into a real athlete, and I started running and doing races in the summertime. I started bodybuilding—I wanted to be strong. When you work your body, it makes you feel more powerful. And this was after a lifetime of not doing a thing. Before that I said, 'Give me high heels and point me to the Plaza.' I played Miss Lady. People from my earlier life still don't believe I'm an athlete."

Since then Gertie has become an avid skier and has skied throughout the United States and Europe. And she's gotten into other sports, including tennis, running, and biking. She goes on multiday bike trips all over the world.

A GOOD REASON TO GO OUT IN WINTER: BURN, BABY, BURN

• • • • • • • • • • • • • • • • • •

All winter sports burn a significant number of calories and are great exercise for keeping healthy and fit. Just being out in the cold makes your body work to keep you warm. Snowshoeing and cross-country skiing are the most aerobic sports and therefore the best workouts.

Martha Harkey started out snowboarding for fun but ended up founding a snowboard apparel company.

Martha Harkey

Martha Harkey is the founder of Yang Snowboard Clothing, a company that started as unisex but switched to women's apparel after Martha saw that no one was making women's snowboard clothing. Before going into the business, she was a pharmacologist on the faculty at Davis School of Medicine, specializing in research. It was her love of snowboarding that made her switch careers for almost ten years.

Martha had been a skier for years, enjoying the mountains and the snow but never skiing much more than a week or two during vacation. In the mid-1980s she started seeing people snowboard and was fascinated. "The first time I saw a woman snowboarding was in 1988," she said. "At that time it seemed as if only adolescent guys were doing it." She had suffered a bad knee injury and heard that snowboarding was easier on the knees, so she decided to give it a try. "I was hooked after my first lesson. I basically spent the day falling down. But it was fun to try something new—that's what stimulated my interest. I'm kind of athletic but not that into sports. When I first started linking turns, I got hooked and started seeking it out." Martha and her husband bought snowboards, and since 1990 they haven't done much else, even going in the summer.

Martha soon noticed their ski clothes were getting wet because they were sitting down a lot. She saw that snowboarders wore street clothes and didn't have really functional, waterproof outfits. "Why don't we try to make snowboard clothing?" she said. And so her company, Yang, was born. "I saw snowboarding as a very exciting sport that was growing very quickly. Starting Yang was something I was really enthusiastic about. I like to do something new and different, even if it's something I know nothing about." Today she has returned to pharmacology, specializing in alternative medicine, but she continues to snowboard as often as she can.

Snowshoeing, winter's easiest sport, can also offer as much of an aerobic workout as you want it to.

MORE REASONS TO GET OUT AND GET MOVING

Avoid winter blues and let the sun shine in

Everyone misses the sun in winter, but many winter resort locations enjoy sunshine most of the season. In the western United States (Colorado, California, New Mexico) and in Europe it's usual to get sunny winter days. And you are almost guaranteed warm and sunny weather in March and April. Besides, it's good to be outdoors—why stop in the winter? Fresh air is always healthy.

Impress your friends

We all love to congratulate ourselves on accomplishing something new. Even I was impressed when a 70-year-old friend told me she went snowshoeing in Vermont one weekend—it sounded so cool. Don't underestimate the "cool" factor of winter sports. No one has to know just how good you are. Think like a guy: they're notorious for tales of wondrous feats on the slopes when they were probably just making ordinary turns. After a venturesome day in the snow, it's fun to sit back with friends and share stories.

Meet new friends

Your entire life can change once you get involved in winter sports. Not only will you meet new friends when you're out skiing or skating, you may even seek out similar people at home. Ski clubs, local ice-skating rinks, and outdoor clubs are all places to make friends and find companions for your next adventure.

Snowshoes can be your entrée to a magical winter landscape.

Family fun

Winter sports are a great way to keep the family together. Everyone has fun. Kids are thrilled by downhill skiing and snowboarding. Even if you're not all at the same level, you can all ski on the same mountain and vacation at the same resort.

Mental therapy

Forget doing yoga and reading about Zen. Being outside in the winter surrounded by beautiful scenery and magical landscapes can put even the most stressed-out mind at peace. All these sports require concentration, and when you're thinking about how to get down the hill or where to make your next turn, you're not thinking about what you forgot to do at the office.

Confidence building

It's uplifting to be outside in the cold, braving and conquering the elements. After you've done something you never thought you'd do, you feel on top of the world. There are so many challenges to overcome, from snowboarding through a blizzard to making it up the hill on cross-country skis without having to take them off and walk. After you're done, you feel a sense of power and superiority as you think, I did that! Anything that's good for you and fun too is hard to beat.

Chapter 2

❄ GETTING STARTED

I've always loved winter. The air is fresh and invigorating, and a romp in the elements gives me a healthy glow. Yet so many people I know resign themselves that once winter starts it's time to stay indoors. Winter can be dark and dreary—especially if you don't look forward to your usual sports. But skiing, snowboarding, snowshoeing, or ice-skating can end all that. Getting outdoors in the cold is exhilarating.

This book will help you learn about the wide range of winter sports options, from the simple pleasure of a laid-back hike through the woods on snowshoes to

"Learning how to ski at 32 was one of the most liberating things I ever did. I was always too scared to try it, but thanks to some incredibly supportive and patient friends, I did it. It was hard and I wasn't always successful, but I stuck with it and enjoyed both the skiing and the boost to my confidence."

—Patricia O'Connell, new skier

the adventurous thrill of a backcountry trek through the wilderness using cross-country skis. Either experience can be yours. First, consider what winter sport you're interested in trying. Sliding downhill might totally intimidate some people but really appeal to others. Trudging up a mountain on

Enjoying a spring **snowshoe** trek on the slopes of Okemo Mountain in Vermont.

snowshoes might strike some as too strenuous but be energizing to others. Gliding through the woods on cross-country skis might seem like a boring chore, but for many it represents a great way to get a good workout in a short time.

OK, so you want to participate in winter sports but you're not sure how to get started. To figure out which sport would be most appealing, consider these questions:

Do you enjoy learning a sport that has a quick learning curve and isn't intimidating? Think about snowshoeing. It's easy to learn and offers plenty of control, so you don't have to worry about sliding or losing your balance.

What do you want to accomplish by taking up a winter sport? If you're primarily after a good workout, consider snowshoeing, ice-skating, or cross-country skiing. All are highly aerobic and offer lots of exercise in a short time.

Do you shy away from hassle? A lot of winter sports do have a big hassle factor, but try not to look at it that way. Everything can be a hassle—even going to the beach if you're the type to pack a chair, a cooler, and a big bag of stuff to do (magazines and such). Snowshoeing and ice-skating are the simplest of the winter sports covered in this book. You can do either of these almost anywhere, and both require minimal equipment. Buy a pair of snowshoes for a hundred dollars or so and keep them in your car trunk so you're ready to go out for a trek whenever the urge strikes you.

Are you looking for thrill and adventure? Consider alpine skiing or snowboarding. Nothing beats the excitement of going downhill. And cross-country skiing and snowshoeing can offer adventure if you go off the beaten track and explore the wilderness.

As you read through the following chapters about these various winter sports, consider these questions and your answers to decide what you want to try this winter.

• •

"**S**kiing is truly a test of your own inner strength, an opportunity to face and conquer your fears. It's just you against the mountain, the cold, and your own belief in yourself. There's nothing quite like looking up at an imposing mogul field that you've just skied, or picking yourself up from a nasty fall just to keep skiing."

—Shannon Entin, publisher of *FitnessLink*, who didn't learn to ski until her senior year of college

• •

WHERE TO FIND OUT ABOUT WINTER SPORTS

If you're like most women interested in winter sports, you probably don't have a clue on how to get started. Don't feel bad—it's not as if you could go the local gym and find out how to snowboard.

Indeed, there are few or no resources guiding women who want to get involved. But once you get in the loop, you'll discover there are special clinics and instruction weeks for women who want to learn or improve their technique in skiing, snowboarding, or snowshoeing. Many women find they're more comfortable learning with other women, and these how-to clinics have grown in popularity. (Check chapter 9, Resources, for specific clinics and information on where to go.) Besides special learning programs, there is now women's equipment for all the winter sports discussed in this book, which also makes it easier to learn them. But most women don't know that women's skis or snowboards exist, so many have been content to use hand-me-downs from their husbands, boyfriends, or even sons. Using the wrong gear is not much fun, and it slows your learning.

One of the best places to look for information is at a ski, snowboard, or outdoor shop. These can be great resources for finding out where to go to skate, ski, snowboard, or snowshoe. Some shops organize bus trips to winter resorts. Or they may have a bulletin board with information and brochures about where to go. Most post daily snow reports, and shop employees can tell you about local areas and the latest conditions, since they usually make it a priority to get out and do the sports they love most.

Although the typical outdoor shop doesn't specialize in winter goods—it's full of camping gear, hiking boots, and clothing—it usually does sell winter clothing, snowshoes, and maybe even cross-country gear. These shops are run by knowledgeable people who can guide you to places to go. Even the local sports shop that specializes in school sports can be helpful, especially if it's family owned or individually managed. This is usually where you'll find ice skates, and employees can direct you to local ice-skating spots. Also, seek out shops that go the extra yard for women and are more sensitive to our needs. Some go all out to cater to women and to create a female-friendly environment. Look for special women's events, which can offer great deals and good advice. For example, one shop in Minneapolis

Shop salespeople will help you determine what equipment is right for you. Here, finding **snowboard boots** that fit well.

holds a "women's only" sale on Super Bowl Sunday every year. Not only is there a 20 percent discount on everything, but women instructors and other female experts are there to answer questions about the merchandise as well as to provide tips on skiing and snowboarding. Cocktails, hors d'oeuvres, and fresh flowers add to the festive atmosphere.

Be wary of employees who are condescending to neophytes: they may discourage you from pursuing your dream. It's important to establish relationships with the salespeople. Let them know what your experience has been and what you're looking for. Before you know it, they may have you signed up for a trip to a nearby winter area.

WHERE TO GO TO GET STARTED

For some winter sports, you can get started right in your hometown unless you live in a warm climate. This is particularly true for ice-skating, snowshoeing, and cross-country skiing. Even warm locations may have an indoor ice-skating rink. Although I grew up in a variety of states with different climates, I skated regularly. When I lived in Chicago, it was easy: it was always cold in winter, and there was always some sort of outdoor rink. In Kentucky things were different, but my mother and I still kept it up, visiting an indoor rink frequently.

Indeed, ice-skating is the best sport to choose if you're looking for something hassle-free and don't want to travel. You can do it almost anywhere, conditions permitting. To find out about ice-skating in your area, check with local parks, municipal centers, and schools. Even if it's not particularly cold, water can be treated to make it freeze. If it is cold, make sure it's been below freezing for long enough that lakes, ponds, and canals are completely frozen. Then you can choose your spot. Like solitude? You can probably find a small pond or even a creek in the woods. Want company? Try the local, town-organized rinks. Often they'll provide a fire and some shelter, which can be a welcome break on really cold days and nights.

Persistence pays when it comes to finding a place to ski or skate in areas with unreliable weather. Outdoor enthusiast Susan Oostdyke manages to find snow even during the warmest New Jersey winters by heading into the northern hills of Green Pond. Even when there's no sign of snow in most of New Jersey, she finds some there on the highest hills. She takes her cross-country skis and forges her own trail on old fire roads at the top of a mountain ridge. If it hasn't snowed, she'll even take her skis out on

The only equipment you need to **ice skate** are skates—and ice. Even if your town doesn't have a formal ice-skating rink, there might be a pond that's perfect for skating.

a frozen lake, or sometimes she'll opt for ice-skating. "I can go skiing right out my back door into the fields and the woods. I used to go every morning with my mother before work," Susan recalls. "It's energizing. I find peace and solitude in the woods. It lifts your spirits for the rest of the day."

Snowshoeing and cross-country skiing are also easy-access sports since they can be done almost anywhere when there's snow on the ground. But if it's skiing or snowboarding you're after, you'll have to visit a mountain resort. Of course you don't have to go to the world-famous resorts of Vail or Aspen or Killington to get started—you can visit a small area. Some places might be closer to home than you think. And don't be discouraged by warm weather or lack of snowfall. A little bit of elevation can make a big difference in snowfall and cold, and most resorts also make their own snow. Snowmaking has become

Top: Small resorts are ideal for teaching children to ski or snowboard because of the uncrowded slopes and friendly atmosphere. Here, the author is with her nephew, Rory.
Bottom: Like cross-country skiing, **snowshoeing** can be done almost anywhere there's snow.

so sophisticated that some systems don't even require freezing temperatures.

Small resorts are ideal places to begin skiing or snowboarding. They cost less, they're easier to get around, and they're friendly. There may even be one near you. Consider this little known fact: New York is the state with the most ski areas, followed by Michigan, Wisconsin, and California, though most people would guess Colorado, Vermont, or Utah.

Another way to find out about local ski resorts is to contact some of the industry organizations for information. Both the National Ski Areas Association and SnowSports Industries America (SIA) have Web sites with helpful information. (See chapter 9 for Web sites and phone numbers.) SIA's Snowlink is particularly extensive and can tell you about retail shops and ski areas in your region, learn-to-ski and learn-to-snowboard programs, where to snowshoe or cross-country ski, and details on products. If you need more information, this Web site also has links to

"**I**'ve found cross-country skiing a wonderful way to exercise in winter. . . . It's a great way to enjoy the outdoors without the commitment of a full day (and, face it, the expense) needed for downhill skiing."

—Tamsin Venn, publisher of *Atlantic Coastal Kayaker*

ski resorts and gear manufacturers. Resort links will list programs and special events happening at the area all year long. Almost all post daily snow reports, and some show a daily picture so you can see what the conditions are really like.

FINDING OUT MORE ABOUT WINTER SPORTS

Magazines and books about skiing, snowboarding, cross-country skiing, and snowshoeing can also be good resources for information on where to go and where to find the deals. Magazines like *Skiing* and *Ski* typically publish a "resort guide" every fall. These guides list resorts and provide information about the activities and services the areas offer. They also tell you which resorts are better for families, for singles, for beginners, and so on. (You'll find more on specific magazines in chapter 9.)

Ski and snowboard clubs are another source of information, and they can be a great way to save money. Many have their own winter chalet or house in snow country and charge a small fee for lodging (from $20 a night to $80 a weekend). Meals are family style, and everyone helps clean up at the end, keeping the prices down. In addition, the members can get lift tickets at a group rate and substantially less than what you'd pay at the ticket window. The only problem: clubs are like underground networks. They're difficult to find out about because many are run by members and are listed only by the leader's name. Resorts may know of some clubs, and the Internet lists some. Clubs specifically for snowshoeing and cross-country skiing are rare, but outdoor shops may know of sources. Check out bike or running clubs, which may organize snowshoeing and cross-country trips in the winter. (See the resource guide in chapter 9 for specific information on clubs.)

Ski and snowboard swaps are also a good way to locate people who know all about winter sports. Enthusiastic skiers and snowboarders are only too happy to talk about the sports they love. At local swaps not only will you get good prices on gear and clothing, but you can meet people who can give you essential information on the best places to go, how to get deals on tickets, and the optimal time to plan your excursion. Although they're called *ski* or *snowboard* swaps, these

"**W**hy do I love it? Well, what's not to love? Skiing is a sport that takes you to the mountains, complete with fresh air, beautiful vistas, and a crisp, cold, clean environment that's completely absent from my otherwise urban lifestyle. And skiing isn't just a sport, it's an experience."

—Christine Gasparac, 29, recreational skier

events also often have cross-country gear and sometimes ice skates. Snowshoes are still a fairly new, hot item, so you won't see them as much at swaps. In chapter 3 you'll find more information on swaps and on how to choose gear.

START OFF RIGHT: TAKE A LESSON

Most resorts now feature women's instructional programs for downhill and cross-country skiing or snowboarding. These clinics range from one day or a weekend to a week. They're taught by female instructors, and all aspects of the sport are covered, including equipment, fitness, nutrition, and other mind and body considerations.

Women's weeks or instructional programs have become popular, particularly for skiing.

Call ahead to the resort you want to visit and ask about packages for beginners. Almost every winter resort in America now offers special deals for new skiers and snowboarders. Prices can range from $20 to $60 for a lesson, lift ticket, and rental gear. This is obviously the way to go, since a lift ticket alone costs between $20 and $60. The price depends on the size of the resort and whether you go midweek or on the weekend. If you can go midweek, do. Not only is it cheaper, but the slopes are less crowded and classes are smaller. This will make your first experience more fun and less intimidating. Many winter resorts also offer cross-country and snowshoe lessons, some with attractive pricing. Several locations also have ice-skating rinks with rentals and lessons.

START EASY AND WORK YOUR WAY UP

Maybe the thought of going downhill is not for you. Or maybe you want a simpler introduction to winter sports. If so, consider snowshoeing or cross-country skiing, both of which are attracting more and more women. They both offer an easy, hassle-free way to get outdoor exercise in the winter. And it doesn't take long to build up a sweat and get a real aerobic workout. Veteran snowshoer Claire Walter says, "Snowshoeing is so easy it's almost embarrassing. Snug the snowshoes onto your feet and start walking. That's all there is to it."

Some women take up cross-country skiing or snowshoeing because they find themselves at a ski or snowboard resort but don't want to go out on the slopes every day. Sue Born, who organizes snowshoe outings for women in Snowmass, Colorado, says: "Couples come out to the Aspen area with the husbands hot to hit the slopes. The women might enjoy that for a day or two, but they're also looking for a more laid-back experience." On Born's outings they might

• •

"My question: What's the best thing about cross-country skiing with a white ponytail? It helps set other middle-aged women free, too. We're the generation who teetered madly at center court trying not to slip over the line and foul at girl's basketball, the ones who were not allowed to run on the school (boys') track. Now we can—and most especially now that we've lost the inhibitions of youth. Who cares what we look like? We're doing what we want!"

—Starr Ackley, 51, avid cross-country skier

• •

spend half a day snowshoeing, then have a gourmet lunch in a beautiful spot. One nice aspect of cross-country skiing and snowshoeing is that you can make them as easy or as strenuous as you want. And you don't have to be in great shape. It does take some basic level of fitness, however. If you'd find a mile's walk tough, chances are you'll get tired after five or ten minutes of cross-country skiing or snowshoeing. A person with little physical endurance would do best sticking to a flat area and not venturing too far. But if you're a runner, biker, or skater, you could easily handle a longer trek.

Women try cross-country skiing for reasons other than rounding out a resort experience, too. Veteran winter sports participant Mary Robinson loves the solitude of the sport. "I love cross-country skiing because of the silence—it's just me and the snow and the trees and the sky. I like that it requires a lot of exertion. I like sports where I compete only with myself."

Tamsin Venn, publisher of *Atlantic Coastal Kayaker* magazine and mother of two, goes cross-country skiing to keep in shape in the winter. "I've found cross-country skiing a wonderful way to exercise in winter. I need a large dose of aerobic exercise at least three times a week for my sense of well-being. I can go out for a few hours—either at a cross-country center or into the wild woods of New Hampshire with my hyper spaniel—get a good workout with no pounding of the joints, enjoy the blessed silence and wind in the winter trees, and get back home in time for the children's (ages 2 and 5) lunch. My husband's still not too grouchy yet with babysitting duties. Now it's his turn. And the dog is calmed down. It's a great way to enjoy the winter outdoors without the commitment of a full day (and, face it, the expense) needed for downhill skiing (which I also thoroughly enjoy).

"However, we did buy a pulk [a type of sled] several years ago to pull the children around the cross-country centers we go to. We figured it was easier than trying to rent one each time. The pulk in itself has been a way for all of us to enjoy skiing together. We just don't ski too far from the warming hut and are prepared for frequent hot chocolate breaks and missing mittens."

Unlike downhill skiing or snowboarding, it doesn't take long to get comfortable on cross-country skis or on snowshoes. And that's one of the great things about it. A beginner can reach the same beautiful terrain as an expert; the beginner just moves slower. Once you get comfortable sliding on cross-country skis or trekking uphill on snowshoes, you may find you want to tackle downhill skiing or snowboarding.

GET IN SHAPE

All skiers and snowboarders are familiar with aching legs and burning thighs during and after their first day out. Then they wise up and make sure they exercise before they hit the slopes next time to make their experience easier and more fun. Before the winter sets in or before you go on your trip, plan to do a little preseason conditioning. If you're in shape, you'll be less tired and less likely to injure yourself. You'll also improve your performance. One of my best seasons skiing was the year I went in-line skating a lot during the summer and fall. In-line skating is an excellent way to train for both downhill and cross-country skiing as well as for ice-skating, because you use many of the same muscles and balance techniques. When I hit the slopes in December that year, there was plenty of powder—as luck would have it. Snow like that is great, but skiing it takes real power, especially when it's deep. Powder is something you wish for after you've had a few days or weeks of building up your ski muscles. But that year I skied it unbelievably well. I was perfectly centered and balanced over my skis, and I had the strength to turn when and where I wanted. I credit that to the in-line skating I did. When I feel really inspired, I like to exercise for several weeks before ski season. But it pays to do at least something, even if it's just a couple of days before you go.

This easy exercise doesn't require any equipment but provides good stretch to your upper thigh. Pull your leg gently and slowly until you feel the stretch in your upper thigh.

Here's my favorite recipe for getting in shape for the winter, borrowed from my days on the Rutgers Ski Team. Even though it's geared to downhill skiing, it offers a good basic workout that will make your first day at any of the winter sports a little less strenuous. Use this as a guideline or make up your own exercise regime out of something you like to do, whether it's yoga, swimming, or power walking.

Start the fall off right with a dryland training regime beginning in mid-September or so. Plan to exercise at least twice a week, ideally three times. Sessions can vary from twenty minutes to an hour and a half. The important thing is to get out and do something.

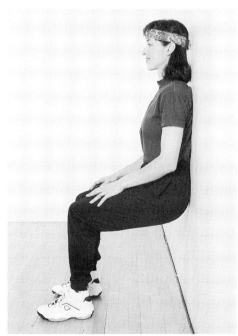

The **wall-sit** is a good, thigh-strengthening exercise. Downhill ski racer Lisa Feinberg Densmore demonstrates, with calves parallel to the wall and your thighs parallel to the floor.

Lateral jumps are a good way to develop a rhythm you can apply to snowboarding or downhill skiing.

Begin the workout with some basic stretching exercises that you're probably already familiar with. Start with some warm-up stretches like lunges, toe and arm stretches, and neck rolls. Move on to stretches that work your hamstrings and your quadriceps as well as your inner and outer thighs. Here are some suggestions: Sitting with your legs stretched out in front, reach for your ankles; spread your legs apart and reach for your toes; while standing, pull your ankle back toward your rear to stretch your thigh; squat with knees spread out and reach for your ankles; sit with soles touching to stretch your inner thighs. A more vigorous thigh exercise is to sit on an

"I think what I always liked about downhill skiing was that it's a personal challenge. I liked the speed, and as scared as it sometimes made me, I loved how I felt when I made it down—strong and powerful and capable. I loved using my muscles, being sore and tired yet exhilarated at the end of the day. I guess I really like sports where I'm immersed in nature at the same time. . . . I think the great thing about individual sports like skiing and cross-country skiing . . . is that they allow you to be completely in the moment—they require all your attention, focus, and senses. Everything else goes out of your head. . . . I love that aspect of it."

—Veteran winter participant Mary Robinson, grant writer

imaginary chair against the wall. Start out by holding the position for one minute, gradually increasing to three to five minutes.

To stretch the calves, push against the wall with your arms and stretch one leg back (keeping your heel on the floor). Stretch your back by lying flat and lifting your legs up and back over your shoulders, or as far as you can. Do this slowly, feeling the stretch throughout your back.

After you've warmed up, do some sort of aerobic exercise. Running is ideal. Try to go at least ten minutes, eventually working up to twenty or twenty-five. Include some backward running, excellent for working the upper thighs.

When you finish, you can move on to a few power stretch exercises. Squat jumps work the upper and lower legs. Start by squatting with your arms in front, bent ninety degrees at the elbow. Spring upward and land on your toes, using your knees to absorb the impact. Next try lateral jumps. Jump sideways rhythmically from one leg to the other. Jumping rope is also excellent for developing eye and foot coordination as well as building muscles. A workout is not complete without some abdominal exercises like leg crunches and sit-ups. End your session with some easy stretching to relax your body.

Of course, there are many activities that can help you get in shape, including biking, in-line skating, hiking, and running. If you belong to a gym with a NordicTrack, try it: it's an excellent machine that works the upper as well as the lower body. It mimics cross-country skiing and is an ideal training method for the sport. Weight training is great for building strength in your legs; try leg presses, squats, leg extensions, and leg curls.

Chapter 3

STAYING WARM: CLOTHING, ❄ ACCESSORIES, AND GEAR

Comfort is the key element to keep in mind when picking out your outfit. Winter can be very pleasant —even if you *hate* the cold—once you learn to dress properly.

I bought my first real ski outfit when I was in high school—on sale at a local sporting goods warehouse sale for about $65. That red getup became my signature look, and I wore it through most of my college years.

But it wasn't always great. When I went to my first race camp with the ski team, we skied in the rain the entire first day. I don't know if waterproof-breathable garments had even been invented at that point. I had to figure out a way to dry all my clothing for the next morning, when temperatures dropped considerably. I was so envious of the more experienced girls who had more than one outfit.

Yet while having more than one outfit is nice, it can be impractical, especially when traveling. Who wants to lug all that stuff around? To this day I'm a one-outfit person. But that one outfit is versatile and protects me from the elements even when the conditions change drastically.

Thanks to advancements in outdoor apparel technology in the past twenty years, there are lots of choices available, depending on your needs. Yes, it's a bit of an investment; as with any clothing, prices can vary depending on how fancy you want to go. On average, depending on your tastes, you can pay anywhere from $150 to $800 to get everything you need for the winter. Ski and snowboard outfits will cost more than clothing suitable for cross-country skiing and snowshoeing. But once you're geared up, you can use the same stuff for years. And technical winter clothing—pieces that repel and wick away moisture—can be worn not only for your playtime in the snow but also for a trip to the grocery store or a night on the town. It will keep you warm!

Pick a comfortable outfit that will keep you warm.

Buying used clothing is another possibility. Ski and snowboard swaps, consignment shops (especially in resort towns), classifieds, and tag sales can all be sources for good-quality used winter clothing. The swaps are a wonderful place to shop, and prices can range from $5 to $300; the higher prices are usually new items that the swaps bring in from local shops. There are some places that actually rent clothing, but those are few and far between, though it may be a trend to look out for.

Comfort is the key element to keep in mind when picking your outfit. Winter can be very pleasant—even if you *hate* the cold—once you learn to dress properly. And that's easy when you fill your wardrobe with a few necessary basics, including quality accessories like socks, gloves, and hats. The layering concept is the best way to ensure comfort outside in the winter, when conditions can vary from one hour to the next.

LAYERING: IT'S AS EASY AS 1-2-3

Layering is the big buzzword in the winter outdoor world, but don't let an overzealous salesperson confuse you with technical jargon. How many times have you listened to someone babble on about Gore-Tex and moisture transport systems and wicking? There are so many terms that it can be overwhelming even to the experienced shopper. The basic idea behind proper dressing is to keep warm in cold conditions and stay dry if it turns warmer or if your body heats up during your workout.

A layered outfit is typically made of three pieces: the innermost layer next to the skin (long underwear), the middle layer (microfleece knit), and the outermost layer (a shell). Each component has been constructed to help athletes maintain a stable body temperature while exercising outdoors.

Layering is practical because you can add or remove layers depending on the temperature and conditions and on how hard you're exercising. It's a very popular way to dress because it's the best way to obtain a near-perfect combination of waterproofness, windproofness, insulation, and breathability according to your own metabolism. An insulated parka combines all these elements in one piece, so there's not much opportunity for temperature regulation unless it has vents.

When you go to a sports shop you may or may not get someone who's knowledgeable about

SPECIALTY SHOPS: A GREAT PLACE TO BEGIN

• • • • • • • • • • • • • • • • • •

Specialty shops are a natural place to begin your journey into the world of winter. Whether it's a store that specializes in downhill skis, snowboards, or outdoor gear (including snow-shoes and cross-country skis), these merchants take the extra step for their customers. Many are family-run and have employees who love the sport. They're happy to answer your questions and help educate you about the sport you're seeking to try. In fact, most good specialty stores double as centers for information on skiing, snow-shoeing, or snowboarding. Some even run trips to the mountains. These shops can also be good sources for used equipment, and some organize swaps during the off-season.

how to put your outfit together. For the best place to shop, look for a specialty retailer—a shop that specializes in gear for skiing, snowboarding, cross-country skiing, or other outdoor sports. Here you'll find salespeople who are most likely enthusiastic about sports and more than willing to answer your questions (if you're lucky, in simple terms).

Getting outfitted for winter sports shouldn't be like buying a new car. Equip yourself with a few terms and understand what you're trying to accomplish before you go to the store. Then you'll be able to cut through the sales pitch and find good-quality apparel without breaking your bank account. Here's a brief description of what you need to know about each layer.

Basic layer: underwear

No matter what sport you plan to take up, long underwear is a must. The first or inner layer tends to be made of a light-weight, thin fabric that will keep you dry and warm by wicking the moisture away from your skin. However, not all first layers are thin and lightweight; various

Avoid cotton in **base-layer clothing**. The right fabric and a good fit are necessary for comfort.

weights are available depending on how much insulation and warmth you're looking for. Still, as the technology gets more and more sophisticated, even the thicker fabrics are lighter than ever before.

Most long underwear is made of synthetic, high-tech polyester weaves, but silk continues to be popular because of its natural wicking capacity and its unbeatable comfort. And while cotton is definitely passé (it's slow to dry once it gets wet), wool underwear has made a comeback because wool is a natural wicker. And the wool used now (usually merino) is treated so it doesn't shrink or make you itch. The main criterion for all long underwear fabrics is that they must be quick-drying and pull moisture away from the skin and through the fabric, acting as an evaporation system.

There are many options to wear beneath the first layer of long underwear, from active sports bras to sporty briefs in

• •

My simple, go-anywhere outfit is made up of three layers: long underwear top and bottom, lightweight and stretchy fleece zip turtleneck, unlined shell, and unlined pants. If that's not enough I add a heavier fleece pullover or just substitute a heavier fleece top for the lightweight one. On really cold days I add a down vest to the mix. On the bottom half I usually survive with just long underwear beneath the shell pants, sometimes opting for heavier weaves if the temperature's in the single digits or lower. My legs move the most, so they don't get as cold as my upper body.

• •

comfortably light and airy weaves. New briefs range from ultralight meshes to heavier weaves, but all are lighter or the same weight as a typical pair of Hanes cotton undies. It's not necessary to use underpants and bras designed specifically for sports, but it makes sense that all pieces next to the skin should be capable of drawing the moisture away.

Long underwear itself has gotten so fancy it can hardly be called underwear anymore. Also known as sports performance wear, the pieces can double as multifunctional sports apparel, with styles ranging from tights and pants to turtleneck and crewneck tops. Possibilities abound: a base layer, like lightweight microfleece tights, is designed to double as running tights. For example, Duofold makes tights that combine CoolMax and Pontetorto fleece, designed with a wide waistband and flat seams for a sleek cut, giving a sporty look good enough to wear anywhere.

Don't get confused by all the brand names. The hangtags on the garments reveal that the materials are all designed to do pretty much the same thing. Fabrics from Dupont such as ThermaStat and CoolMax are common and are used to make many different brands of underwear, but many manufacturers use their own brand-name fabrics. Some of the more popular names include Lowe Alpine's Dryflo, Patagonia's Capilene, Marmot's DriClime, and Terramar's Transport. Each type of fabric is woven or knitted differently, but all are designed to disperse mois-

Microfleece is popular for **middle-layer clothing** because of its insulating qualities and light weight.

ture by pulling it through the fabric so it can evaporate. Stretch components are also being added to permit close-fitting styles without bulk. Whether you decide to go with synthetics or natural fibers, always base your final decision on fit and comfort.

Middle layer: insulation

The middle layer is for insulation and is made of a medium-weight fabric. These fabrics are designed to trap warm air between their fibers. Polyester microfleece has become popular because it's lightweight and cozy. It also blocks the wind and dries quickly if it gets wet.

Malden Mills popularized microfleece when it introduced Polartec, which comes in a variety of weights and types. Variations on this basic fleece include Malden's Power Stretch, which adds four-way stretch to the wicking and breathability. Some high-tech fleeces can be used as an outer layer, especially when combined with a windproof and waterproof shield like Gore's Windstopper. As the basic fleece style matures, look for more and more variations. Designers are weaving patterns into the fabrics for a different look or adding technical features like stretch. Excellent fleece products are available under several brand names, such as L.L. Bean, Lowe Alpine, Patagonia, and Sierra Designs.

Because the more strenuous winter sports of snowshoeing and cross-country skiing make you sweat so much, it's crucial to dress properly if you plan to pursue these sports. For these sports, fleece is excellent. Not only does it provide insulation, but it wicks moisture to the outside. The more you sweat, the more it wicks, so when you stop moving you'll be warm and dry. For instance, if you're hiking on snowshoes to the top of a mountain, you'll sweat on the way up and might want to strip off a layer or open the vents on your shell or fleece top. Once you stop, however, you'll cool down rapidly and need to put on more layers to stay warm. And, you'll need a garment that dries quickly.

For less strenuous sports like skiing and snowboarding where you're riding a lift and not exerting as much energy, you'll need to wear a shell or jacket over that layer of fleece. Many women also choose a shell or jacket with an insulating layer like Thermoloft or down built in or containing a thin layer of synthetic insulation that offers warmth but with a slimmer silhouette. Primaloft is a synthetic down that is less expensive and dries faster than real down.

Most brands now offer some sort of layering system with multifunctional pieces designed to coordinate so that a fleece layer or down vest can be zipped into an outer shell. The Marmot brand offers many layering options, and the company is especially good at women's designs thanks to designer Neide Cooley, who started the effort because she wanted ski clothing that fit her small frame.

Outer layer: protection

The ideal outer layer is made of a fabric that is waterproof or water repellent as well as wind-proof yet still breathable. The main term you'll hear is *waterproof-breathable* (WPB), meaning that the material is waterproof on the outside but lets the steamy interior heat and moisture pass through. Old-fashioned nylon products are waterproof, but they're not breathable; thus they

Snowboard jackets have become very technical to guard against the elements, but they're stylish enough to wear anywhere.

can feel clammy because the vapor from perspiration can't get out and condenses on the inside.

It's not easy to achieve a product that's both waterproof and breathable. W. L. Gore was the first to try it when the company invented Gore-Tex in the early 1980s. Since then many more

high collar for
wind protection

hood stows
in collar

covered placket
for warmth

longer zip pulls
for ease with
gloves

pit zips for
ventilation

zipped chest
pockets

lift ticket clip

Velcro wrist
closure

waterproof-
breathable fabric

hip drawcord

zippered pockets

waterproof-
breathable fabric

built-in gaiters

cuffed ankles

Left: A good **winter jacket** has a water-resistant or waterproof-breathable outer, a zip-off or stowable hood, pockets with zippers in strategic locations (inside and outside), and well-sealed systems at sleeve openings. **Right: Winter pants** should be water-resistant and should have pockets and built-in gaiters to keep snow out. Above all, they should fit well.

manufacturers have followed suit, and there are several brand names to consider, including Ultrex, Gore-Tex, Sympatex, and Entrant as well as dozens of clothing manufacturers' own names like Columbia's Omni-Tec, Marmot's MemBrain, or Lowe Alpine's Triple Point.

All are designed to block out snow or rain yet allow sweat or moisture to escape. Different formulas are used. A fabric's waterproof-breathability property can be microporous—with tiny holes that allow water vapor to pass through—or monolithic, which passes vapor through a solid layer by a chemical process. It can be achieved by a laminate (a waterproof layer bonded to the inside of the fabric) or a WPB coating. A water-repellent finish is often added on top of the WPB shell for additional protection against the elements and to prevent the outside of the fabric from soaking. Also, it helps prevent staining.

Do they work? They all work reasonably well. Hard-core product testers will tell you that the more waterproof a product, the less breathable it is. But it also depends on how active you are. Most will do what they're meant to do: keep you dry and comfortable. Although it's impossible to test a garment's waterproofness and breathability in a store unless you happen to have a portable shower, you can choose a product based on certain visible design features such as seam sealing, wrist closures, and other details that prevent water from penetrating.

Alternatives to the traditional heavier shells are the lighter-weight windbreakers made from fabrics like Gore's Activent, which are water and wind resistant and highly breathable. Another development is a fabric called Dryskin Extreme (developed by a Swiss textile firm called Schoeller); it's a stretchy, woven fleece blend of Cordura nylon, Lycra, and CoolMax designed to keep your skin dry even after hours of intense activity. Its superior wind- and water-proof qualities make it hardy enough to be worn as an outer shell, and its sleek, fitted look makes it downright stylish.

These alternatives are ideal for snowshoeing, cross-country skiing, and other highly aerobic sports. The fabrics protect at various levels of activity. Many stuff into compact little packages that are easy to carry in a backpack.

ACCESSORIES

The winter world is just like the world of fashion; the best outfit in the world isn't much good if you don't have the right accessories. Case in point: you might have the warmest, driest clothes, but if it's snowing like crazy and you don't have goggles, you won't be able to see and you'll be forced to go in. I encountered a woman who was wearing only sunglasses while skiing in a snowstorm. Snow was coming down at a furious rate and it was foggy, making it even harder to see. She'd make a couple of turns and then stop to wipe her glasses, which were wet on the outside and fogging up on the inside. She was nervous and asked me the way to the bottom. I told her I'd ski down with her and lent her my goggles. I couldn't see through her glasses either, but I've skied in snowstorms many times and could "feel" my way down. If I hadn't been there, it would have taken her hours to get down.

Sunglasses and goggles

For any daytime, outdoor activity in winter you should have eyewear that offers protection from damaging ultraviolet rays. If you're skiing or snowboarding you'll want to add a pair of goggles to your winter sports kit. You never know when you might need them. One woman I met thought she'd be fine without because the day started out only partly cloudy. But in the mountains the weather can change fast, so it's best to be prepared for everything. Unless it's a completely cloudless day and the weather forecast is for sun, sun, sun, take the goggles. I usually bring both sunglasses and goggles. If it's sunny, I wear the goggles wrapped around my hat and just use the glasses. If the light gets funky (late afternoon), I put the goggles on. Goggles shield your face from the wind: it can be warm at midday but cold in the early morning and late afternoon. Goggles also add another element of protection by shielding the eyes from injury.

Sunglasses (top) offer protection from dangerous UV rays. Goggles (bottom) offer more protection to the general eye area; some models have interchangeable lenses for different light conditions.

If you're primarily going to be snowshoeing, cross-country skiing, or ice-skating, you can probably get by with just sunglasses. There are many types of goggles and glasses on the market. Each brand has its own secret formula to prevent fogging, but all strive to do the same thing: manage airflow to help the antifog coating dissipate the moisture inside while keeping air turbulence from irritating your eyes. Goggles with double lenses will fog less than those with single lenses. Sunglasses with a wrap style, covering more of your face, are a good choice for snowshoeing or cross-country skiing, since they'll also protect your eyes during a light snowfall.

Goggles also come with different lens colors for sunny, foggy, or flat light conditions. Try to find a lens that works in a variety of conditions or buy extra lenses that pop into the frame. Some sunglasses also come with interchangeable lenses.

Style is another consideration. Many sunglasses and goggles have gone to wider frames for better peripheral and downward vision. Other points to consider are how light the frame is, comfort features like nose pads and soft lining around the edges, and fit. (Are they too small or big? Do the glasses slip down when you move vigorously?) Effective sun protection is a given these days, with U.S. standards for eyewear requiring adequate blockage of the sun's dangerous rays.

Goggles can start as low as $25 and go to $150 or more. Some of the more expensive ones have high-tech gizmos like battery-operated fans to dispel fog. Good-quality sunglasses start at about $30 and can go as high as $300 depending on the cachet of the brand name.

The "ideal" **glove** will depend on the sport itself, the fit of the glove, and your internal thermostat. Ditto for socks.

Gloves and socks

Hands and feet usually get cold first. You can have the warmest jacket and pants, but icy hands or feet can send you flying inside for hot chocolate.

Warm, water-resistant gloves or mittens are a priority. If you're doing the more aerobic sports like ice-skating, snowshoeing, or cross-country skiing, opt for a lightweight pair. Even if it's warm and sunny, you'll still need to wear gloves or mittens when skiing or snowboarding to protect your skin from abrasion when you fall down in the snow or from being cut by ski edges. Good gloves or mittens range in price from $25 to $125. Even the $25 gloves can keep you warm and dry. The more expensive gloves use stronger nylon shells, so they last longer, and they tend to have more bells and whistles. Many winter gloves are made of synthetics like nylon and microfibers (very soft), but leather gloves are still popular with some athletes. I swear by my down-filled leather mittens on colder days.

No matter how warm your gloves or mittens are, some days are so cold you'll need heat packs—disposable inserts that you wear next to your skin. They cost from $1.50 to $4, or you can buy them in bulk at a discount shop or warehouse club. Once opened, they'll generate heat for up to eight hours. There are inserts for your boots, too.

What you wear on your feet is important. Pick socks with a fiber that wicks; otherwise your feet will sweat and then get chilled. Cotton socks are not a good choice—they retain moisture, which can lead to frostbite. It's important to choose socks that fit properly. Make sure they don't wrinkle, or they can cut off your circulation or cause chafing.

Modern sports socks feature good thermal properties, moisture control, odor resistance, proper fit, and comfort. What works best for you depends on how much you perspire, how cold your feet get, the fit you like, and the temperatures you encounter. I prefer thin, close-fitting socks. Like long underwear, socks come in many fiber choices including synthetics, wool, silk, and combinations. I find silk and wool combinations warmer and more comfortable. Merino wool socks are also nice.

Hats, headbands, and neck gaiters

Perhaps you've heard that 50 percent or more of your body heat escapes through your head. No matter what the actual percentage is, you'll stay warmer if you wear a hat or at least protect your ears. Hats for cross-country skiing and snowshoeing tend to be lighter than ski or snowboard hats, but all are getting lighter than the heavy knits of yesteryear. For the coldest temperatures, wear both a hat and a neck gaiter (usually made of a soft, fleecelike fabric). Headbands work well when the temperature's in between. And if it's warm, a baseball hat shields you from the sun a little.

There are lots of choices in hats these days: wool hats with no-itch or fleece liners; fleece hats; chenille hats. Hats can be fun, too, with styles ranging from the pillbox look to beanie styles to cloches. Some designs can be worn as either a hat or a headband. There are even hats with built-in headphones for portable stereos. More high-tech hats include styles with Lycra for stretch or Gore-Tex Windstopper for wind protection. We all know "hat head" can be a pain. Who wants to have rumpled hair at the end of the day? Best advice: don't waste time fixing your hair before you go out.

Helmets

Helmets have become more popular in recent years. Many snowboarders wear helmets, and more and more skiers are donning them, as well. Some mothers put their children in helmets before taking them to skate on the local pond. Simply put, a helmet adds a measure of protection for a day on the slopes or at the rink. Helmets can be worn instead of hats, and in most cases they keep you warmer. Some provide venting in case it gets too steamy. Fit is the crucial

With the variety of winter hats on the market, *everybody* can find a good fit.

Only a helmet that fits well can afford adequate protection. This **helmet** is only one of many styles available to snowboarders, skiers, and ice-skaters.

EQUIPMENT DOS AND DON'TS

• • • • • • • • • • • • • • • • •

- **Be honest about your ability with the salesperson or rental assistant.** You don't want to end up with skis that are too long or ice skates that are too technical.

- **Don't borrow gear from a friend or buy gear at a garage sale.** It's important to have suitable equipment. If you're a beginner, you don't need skis meant for an expert.

- **Always take boots inside at night.** If you leave them in the car they'll freeze by morning. This goes for all types of boots, though alpine ski boots and snowboard boots take the longest to thaw out. Keep them in a warm spot overnight so they're warm and dry by the time you put them on.

element; a helmet mustn't be too big or too small. Also, make sure your vision isn't obstructed. Some helmets are easier to hear through than others. Generally, prices range from $90 to $180, with helmets sporting fancier graphics fetching more.

Sunscreen

Always wear sunscreen when exercising in the winter. At higher altitudes it's even more important; on warmer days your face and ears can fry, so choose a formula with a high SPF (sun protection factor). Some people are so sun-sensitive or have gotten burned so badly that they wear a white layer of zinc oxide smeared all over their faces. Sun reflected off snow is even stronger.

GETTING GEAR

There are many options for getting outfitted with the proper equipment. You can buy new or used gear, or you can rent or demo (try demonstration equipment) when first starting out. I have covered much of the sport-specific gear in the chapters that follow. This section gives some general advice about investing in gear for winter sports.

Certainly if you plan to do a lot of snowshoeing or cross-country skiing it's advantageous to buy your own gear. Equipment for these sports doesn't cost that much—snowshoes start at $100, and L.L. Bean sells cross-country packages with skis, boots, and bindings starting at $200. And it's nice to have your own stuff ready to go so you can take to the trails in your own town—backyard, bike trails, golf course, or whatever. There are far more places to snowshoe and ski cross-country than to rent the equipment.

For your first few times on the slopes, you're better off renting snowboard or ski gear. Many resorts have the latest equipment in their rental shops, and you'll be able to test things like length, board or ski type, and style of boots and bindings while you're deciding whether you like the sport.

Once you've rented a few times and know you want to stick with your new winter sport, you might want to demo a variety of brands to narrow down your choices. This is especially a good idea when buying skis or snowboards. Luckily, most resorts now offer demo equipment, which costs more than standard rentals, with the latest new gear on the market.

Perhaps you're on a budget and don't want to spend a lot of money. You could wait until the end of the season when products are typically marked down or look for swaps in the off-season at local schools, shops, or winter resorts. But if you can't wait, you may find a good buy even during the season. For example, a medium-priced ski package with bindings and boots can range from $350 to $500, which really isn't bad considering it's easy to spend $100 on dinner for two or $200 on a cocktail dress.

WHAT ABOUT GEAR JUST FOR WOMEN?

Then there's the question of whether to buy female-specific equipment. Twenty years ago, equipment made specifically for women was unheard of. And given our history in sports, that's not too surprising. In the late 1960s, women weren't "allowed" to run in the Boston Marathon. In the 1970s, when a couple of women created running clothes specifically for women, they were laughed at and told, "Women don't need special clothes for running." But they persevered, and their company, Moving Comfort, is now one of the leaders in that category.

. . . .

It makes sense to choose products meant for women. Boots are built on female-specific lasts with features like narrower heel pockets. Boards and skis are lighter and easier to turn. Some expert female skiers or riders may not need those characteristics, but they work especially well for novices.

. . . .

BOOT FIT TIPS

- Try on several pairs for comparison's sake.
- Wear only one pair of light- or medium-weight socks.
- Make sure the boot fits snugly—you shouldn't be able to lift your heel very far when the boot is closed.
- Consider buying a footbed or orthotic for a more customized fit.

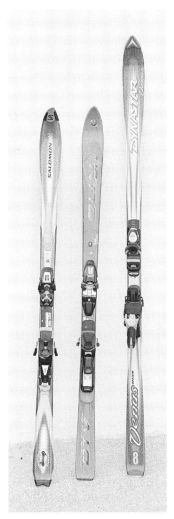

Women's skis are not just paint jobs anymore—they feature a specific design to make turning easier for women.

Similarly, in the 1980s and early 1990s, as women proposed the idea of women's winter sports equipment, many people scoffed. And at first it *was* just marketing hype, especially in the ski market. Not too long ago, in most categories women's equipment was merely men's equipment with a different paint job, usually white or some shade of pink because the male marketers assumed that's what women wanted.

In the 1990s, though, things started to change. Real design and technological differences were made in ski boots and skis to address women's different physiology and needs. Cross-country ski boots and snowboard boots for women got better, too, and by the late 1990s women's snowshoes started showing up.

Snowboards were always a different story. Still a relatively new sport, snowboarding really became popular only in the 1990s. By then, specific equipment for women in several sports was no longer a strange thing. Snowboard companies named boards after pro riders and designed the models according to what that particular rider was looking for, male or female. So all along there were "female" boards— like Burton's Shannon Dunn model or Sims's Tina Basich board. In the late 1990s manufacturers started producing female-specific snowboards. K2 came out with its Luna board, and Morrow introduced the Wildflower series.

It makes sense to choose products meant for women. Boots are built on female-specific lasts with features like narrower heel pockets. Boards and skis are lighter and easier to turn. Some expert female skiers or riders may not need those characteristics, but they work well especially for novices. And you can immediately narrow down your choices by steering to the women's gear.

For more information on specific gear for the sport you're interested in, see the following chapters on skiing, ice-skating, snowboarding, snowshoeing, and cross-country skiing.

Chapter 4

SNOWSHOEING

There's something wonderful about a walk in the woods in wintertime. It's peaceful and serene, and the winter colors seem warm even though it's cold outside. And there are no snakes or ticks or bears to worry about, so you feel you can venture almost anywhere. This is what the sport of snowshoeing is all about—walking on the snow, wherever you want to go.

I love to hike around in the snow with Ban, my yellow lab, at a favorite neighborhood bike trail, which is surrounded by wilderness. I venture off trail and feel the entire forest is my playground. On snowshoes it's easy to just tramp through the open spaces between the trees and explore, happening upon the unusual like a frozen little pond that would have gone undiscovered if I hadn't gone off the beaten track.

A lot of people are falling in love with snowshoeing, one of the hottest rediscovered winter sports. Just put on a pair of snowshoes and off you go. They make it easy to explore anywhere, whether you want to go uphill or across the flats, on ice or through deep snow. And snowshoeing is easy to do—it is truly winter's easiest sport. It's better than just trekking in hiking boots, because

"**S**nowshoeing is really simple and easy—it's like walking, and it's something a nonskier can do."

—Pam Cruickshank, marketing director at Okemo Mountain Resort in Vermont

Snowshoeing can be as as slow-paced as you want.

snowshoes have metal teeth to grip on icy spots and they provide good flotation in fresh snow, so you don't sink up to your knees. As veteran snowshoer and author of *Snowshoeing Colorado* Claire Walter says, "Snowshoes really let you get away from everything and everyone if you want solitude in the backcountry. You don't need to follow a trail. Bushwhacking is acceptable. Unlike cross-country skis, snowshoes don't get caught on the underbrush. The only thing they don't do is glide, so you end up working on both the uphills and the downhills."

Although snowshoeing is probably the world's oldest winter sport—originating between four thousand and six thousand years ago when explorers on snowshoes migrated to new lands—it has just recently become popular again as a winter sport. As early as the eighteenth century, snowshoeing clubs in Québec featured hikes, races, and banquets, and snowshoe outings were popular all over Canada and the United States until the 1930s. Then enthusiasm waned, perhaps eclipsed by more glamorous pursuits like skiing.

In the past decade, however, all that changed with the advent of aluminum and polyurethane snowshoes, some even designed for running in the snow. The snowshoes of today and those of fifteen to twenty years ago are as different as night and day. "People are always saying that the new aluminum-frame snowshoes make the sport so much easier. As much as anything, I think it's the new bindings that helped. They're easy to use and don't freeze up the way the old leather strap versions did," Claire Walter explains. Whatever the reasons, by the late 1990s snowshoeing became the *in* thing to do. It's booming because it's easy and affordable. It also doesn't require any special clothing, and in a few steps you're already "doing it."

You can rent snowshoes for as little as $10 a day at a resort rental shop, at a cross-country touring center, or at ski and snowboard shops. You don't need to spend a fortune. (See pages 55–57 for more details on snowshoes.)

Snowshoeing has become popular for several reasons—for some people it's a way to stay fit and get aerobic exercise in the winter, and for others it offers an easy and quick way to enjoy the outdoors. The stability of snowshoes even makes it possible to carry an infant in a pack without worrying about falling.

Women in particular are taking to snowshoeing in a big way: it's estimated that at least 50 percent of the sport's participants are women. "We get a lot of really sports-minded women who work out regularly at their health clubs in New York, Cleveland, and Miami; they call up and say, 'I want a workout when I come to Vail,' " reports Patricia Hammon, an instructor at Vail's Beaver Creek Snowshoe and Cross-Country Ski Center. "It's an alternative to skiing—either they've had a couple of ski lessons and it's not what they want to do, or their husbands took them up to the top of the black slope and said, 'Come on dear, you can do it,' so they never want to do that again," says Hammon of her clientele. She adds that whereas many of the ski dropouts once just became "condo moms," now they're opting for snowshoeing.

Snowshoeing presents endless possibilities. On a New Year's holiday trip to Vermont one winter when the temperature plummeted to ten below zero (not counting the windchill factor), I elected to go snowshoeing with my dog Ban, on the Long Trail, a hiking path that zigzags its way up the entire length of Vermont. I thought about its advantages over spending the day at a winter resort: it's much cheaper, I won't risk frostbite, I'll get a better workout, and my dog will be happier. Off I went. I did a five-mile hike to the top of the Bromley winter resort, turning back just before I got to the slopes because I didn't want to disturb my communion with nature by mingling with those fast-moving skiers and snowboarders.

Although there wasn't much snow, it was good to have the snowshoes—some parts of the trail had iced up and were steep, but I felt invincible. And I got a great workout.

SNOWSHOEING AT A WINTER RESORT

Wearing snowshoes on the slopes lets you discover a whole new world. Walking on snow is such a different sensation that you experience things you'd never tune in to while rushing down the slopes on skis or a snowboard. Even if you snowshoe on the slopes, you find you don't really notice the skiers and snowboarders whizzing by but focus on nature. If you go to a winter resort, take advantage of services like guides, who can point out things you might not see for yourself: for example, fox tracks are smaller than coyote tracks, and pine trees are different from fir trees. You'd be amazed at the animal tracks you can find just off the trail—look for signs of porcupines, coyotes, foxes, and mice.

But if you've never tried any winter sports, even snowshoeing can be intimidating—especially if you choose to start at a resort, where you may need to take a chairlift. More and more winter resorts are organizing trail networks at the tops of mountains where the snow and views are better. "Women want to be assured they're not going to get hurt and that it's not dangerous," says Hammon, who claims she's never met a woman who couldn't snowshoe. "This is a very easy sport," she tells her clients. "We're going to take a walk; it's like hiking but in the snow." And as an instructor at a resort at high altitude (9,000 to 11,000 feet), she takes special care to make sure her students bring something to drink and use sun protection while out on the trail.

Once women get out and try the snowshoes, says Hammon, it's a different story. "It's so gorgeous and they have so much fun that they say, 'Wow, I'm going to bring my kids tomorrow.' "

The ultimate workout on snowshoes is hiking up a mountain. Snowshoers often use **poles** for stability and balance, especially when walking uphill. Alpine ski poles work best.

GETTING STARTED

There are many aspects to snowshoeing—you can walk, hike, run, or climb. Poles (use alpine ski poles) are optional but are nice as balancing sticks, especially if you're walking in deeper snow or hiking up a hill. Walking is obviously the easiest way to start if you're new to working out or are wary of slippery surfaces. But snowshoes don't slip! Walking on snowshoes is also the way to go if you're breaking your own trail in deep snow. If you're hiking through fresh snow, be sure to choose a snowshoe with a wide platform, which will stay on top of the snow better so you don't have to exert yourself as much.

But if you're an enthusiastic runner, you can choose fitness or running snowshoes and start out jogging. It's a little awkward at first, but once you remember to leave enough space between your feet so the snowshoes don't hit each other, you can get into a nice, steady rhythm. And as technology evolves there are more and more lightweight, aerodynamic snowshoes that make running even easier.

Climbing or hiking up hills is also popular for the ultimate workout. It's getting more and more common to see snowshoe hikers climbing straight up the hill at winter resorts while skiers and snowboarders whiz down the mountain. If you plan to do this, bring plenty of water. There are hydration packs that you wear like a vest; they carry an ample supply and have an easy-to-reach tube for drinking while keeping your hands free. Also, if you've just arrived at a high-altitude location, save the more strenuous workout for a few days later when you've acclimated to the thinner air.

THE BASICS

Even though snowshoeing is easy, there are a few techniques you need to learn. Before starting out, make sure you're properly outfitted so you don't get cold or wet and that you have water so you don't get dehydrated. If you take part in other winter activities, you might have appropriate clothing right in your closet. You can wear running tights or fleece pants with a fleece top if it's not too cold, since you'll be moving a lot and keeping yourself warm. But if you're planning a longer excursion, make sure you have a good layering system. You can buy suitable clothing for $100 to $200 or borrow from a friend when you first try out snowshoeing. (See chapter 3 for more details on apparel.) Always wear sunscreen.

Warming up

It's good to do a few limbering stretches before you start any activity, especially in the cold. This is important for snowshoeing since it may take you a while to warm up by walking. You can do

Do a few basic stretches to warm up before you start off on your hike. Shown here is the **lunge stretch**.

CRAMPON, CLAW, OR CLEAT?

Manufacturers use these three terms interchangeably to describe the metal teeth on the bottom of snowshoes designed to grip into snow. Some will tell you that crampons are more like metal spikes, whereas cleats are metal bars with serrated edges, but the fact is that there are as many kinds of gripping mechanisms as there are snowshoe models.

these stretches indoors, but I recommend doing them outdoors so your body gets adjusted to the temperature while you're limbering up.

Spread your legs in a V and lunge toward your right knee, pushing down on the right thigh. Then do the opposite lunge. Next, still with legs spread, cross your arms over your head and slowly stretch back—not too far, but feeling the arms and back muscles. Then do a simple over-the-head stretch down the side of each leg. Then stand with your legs together and do ten quick jumps with your snowshoes on.

Putting on the gear

Putting on a pair of snowshoes is often trickier than actually snowshoeing. Strapping them on can be confusing—there are so many straps with different loops to put them through that you have no idea where to begin. It's like learning to tie your shoelaces, except it's much harder and there's no rhyme to follow.

Some of the newer snowshoe designs have buckles, but most have a strap-lacing system, often referred to as the *harness* or *binding*. It's important to have the right footwear. Although snowshoes can work with a wide variety of boots, even sneakers,

RIDING THE LIFT
• • • • • • • • • • • • • • • • • • • •

It's true that you can snowshoe almost anywhere—in your backyard, at your neighborhood park, or on a golf course—but more and more winter resorts have organized trail hiking and also can offer snow when there isn't any elsewhere. If you do go to a resort, you'll usually have to use a chairlift.

Getting on and off the chairlift means taking your snowshoes off. Place the bottoms of the snowshoes together so the *crampons* (sharp metal teeth; see diagram) are out of harm's way. Hold the snowshoes in your inside hand. Approach the lift and signal so the lift operator knows you'll be walking onto the lift. When it's your turn, walk quickly to the boarding line and look over your outside shoulder to watch the chair come, using your free hand to steady yourself while you sit down. Then pull the safety bar down (if there is one) and enjoy the ride. At the top, watch for the arrival station (there'll be a warning sign) and get ready to get off—lift the bar up. When the chair gets to the off ramp, step off and walk out of the unloading area quickly. Some chairs run faster than others, but the lift operator at the top is notified that a snowshoer is coming up and will slow the chair down.

When putting on the snowshoe, first line the snowshoe up so the ball of your foot lies at the flex point. Make sure the harness is snug and secure.

it's best to choose comfortable, waterproof hiking boots or snow boots. (And don't forget to wear that warm pair of wicking socks, not cotton. See page 47.)

The *deck* is the main surface of the binding; the *crampon* is located on the bottom, with metal teeth for gripping the snow; and the *frame* is the outside circular metal part (see next page).

The key to putting the snowshoes on properly is to take your time attaching the various straps. First, line the snowshoe up so the ball of your foot lies at the flex point, right between the two components of the harness or binding (see right). The buckle should always be on the outside of the foot. Fasten the front or middle lace or strap first and the heel strap last. Make sure the harness is snug and secure on your foot, but not so tight that it cuts off the circulation. It should feel like your favorite running shoe—once on, you should be able to shake the snowshoe around and not feel any movement. You want to make sure it's snug enough that you won't have to readjust the straps during your hike. If you're running or walking vigorously, the straps will sometimes loosen if they haven't been secured properly. To remove snowshoes, undo the heel strap or buckle first and then loosen the front straps or buckles.

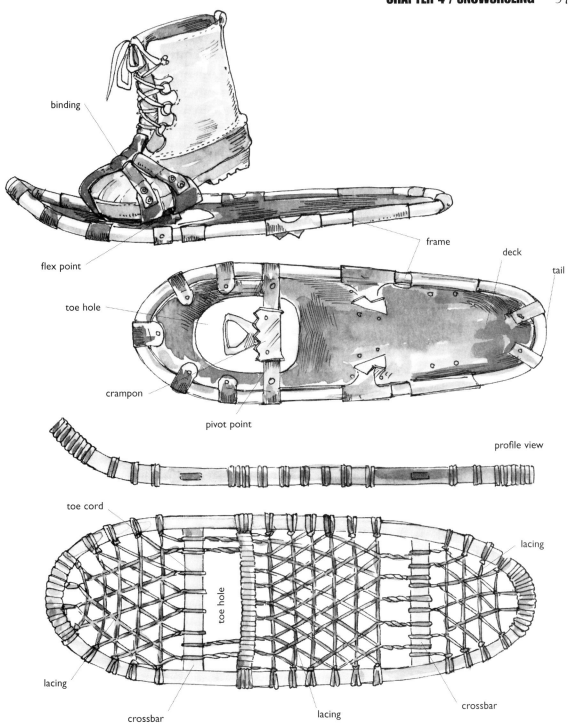

binding

flex point

frame

deck

tail

toe hole

crampon

pivot point

profile view

toe cord

lacing

toe hole

lacing

crossbar

lacing

crossbar

Top: Anatomy of modern snowshoes: tubular frame generally made of aluminum, a deck made of a sturdy, lightweight plastic, a binding with straps or buckles, and crampons for gripping on ice or walking up or down hills. **Bottom:** Traditional snowshoe design accomplishes the same thing but the shoes are made from wood and rawhide or other less high-tech materials.

COMMON CONCERNS

· · · · · · · · · · · · · · · · · · · ·

- **What if I keep step-ping on my other snowshoe?** When snowshoeing, you must lengthen your stride or widen your stance. Exaggerate this in the beginning until you get used to walking with snowshoes on. Eventually you'll develop a sense of where your snowshoes will land so they won't hit each other. Bigger snowshoes are harder to get used to than a smaller, more streamlined design.

- **How will I know if the straps are too tight?** Note whether there are any spots where too much pressure is causing dis-comfort. The snowshoe should be snug, but not so tight that it cuts off your circulation. If your foot begins to tingle or fall asleep, loosen the straps.

(continued next page)

Taking the first steps

Put one foot in front of the other and soon you'll be walking down the snowy path. It sounds simple, and it is. Poles (see page 54) can provide balance and help stabilize your efforts, especially for more intense workouts. They're a must on longer treks—especially into the backcountry or if there's a lot of snow. But when you're learning or if you're just walking around on fairly flat terrain, it's probably easier to keep your hands free and not worry about poles (unless you really want a crutch).

It's best to start out on flat terrain. The pole plant should be opposite the foot plant, so if you move your right foot forward you plant the pole in your left hand, then move your left foot, planting the pole with your right hand in a "diagonal stride." These are natural walking movements; the arm opposite swings with the foot that's stepping forward.

At first the snowshoes might feel a bit awkward—like flip-pers. Use a slightly wider stance than for ordinary walking. Dig in with the *claw* or *cleats* under the front of the snowshoe so that

Use your poles for balance while prac-ticing the **kick turn***.*

you're putting weight on the ball of your foot. This will give you better traction, and you'll feel more stable. Soon you won't notice the snowshoes at all.

Turning

There's one key thing to remem-ber about turning: don't go back-ward. Snowshoes are designed to go forward. If you try to back up the tail will dive into the snow and you might lose your balance and fall. You may succeed at backing up on easier, flat terrain by lifting your feet high and going slowly, but it's awkward and time consuming. Instead, just take a few tiny steps forward in a circle to start turning around.

A *kick turn*, also used in skiing, is another way to turn around and is especially effective on steeper slopes. Place one snowshoe somewhat ahead of the other and plant the pole on that side farther forward, shifting most of your weight onto that leg. Use the other pole to balance. Then lift your rear foot so the tail of the snowshoe points downward and turn it toward the outside so it's facing the opposite direction. Shift the weight to that leg, making sure the snowshoe is firmly planted, then bring the other foot around.

Sidestepping and kick stepping

Sidestepping is walking up the hill sideways. It's a technique used to get up and down steep slopes or to maneuver on icy snow. Although sidestepping is not the preferred method of walking up a hill, it can be useful for getting down, especially if there's a steep, narrow pitch when you have to get through a tricky patch. But the snow needs to be soft or powdery. One of the appeals of snowshoeing over cross-country skiing is that you can just walk up the hill—the claws are designed to minimize backslipping. They grip effectively on hard snow even if the slope is fairly steep.

Still, for some situations it's useful to know how to sidestep. Sidestepping basically requires standing so the snowshoes are crosswise to the mountain—not facing downhill. Step up with the uphill shoe, shifting weight onto it, then bring the downhill shoe parallel to it. Continue making your way up the hill like this.

Going downhill, use the same technique, putting all your weight on one shoe, then the other. As you do this, dig in to make a step of sorts—this is a handy move for steep terrain, icy slopes, and deeper snow.

The preferred method for climbing uphill is called *kick stepping*, or *toe-in*. This requires facing the mountain and climbing straight up. Push or kick the front of the shoe into the slope so it digs into the snow and makes a step. Once the step is stable, lift the other foot and do the same. In new or fresh snow it may take more attempts because the snow may collapse at first. If the slope is steep, dig in farther to make very well defined steps.

COMMON CONCERNS
• • • • • • • • • • • • • • • • • • •

(continued from previous page)

• **What can I do about the snow that keeps flying up the back of my legs?** If you're hiking or walking briskly in a few inches of fresh snow, chances are you'll kick up snow as the back of the snowshoe goes up. Make sure your pants go over the top of your boots, or try tucking them in. If your pants aren't waterproof, wear gaiters over your boots and pants to keep out the snow and ice.

"The new technology is unbelievable. Snowshoes are really lightweight, and they fit snugly to your own boots. The snowshoes made for deeper snow have so much buoyancy it's almost like walking on water. It's great exercise."

—Pam Cruickshank, marketing director at Okemo Mountain Resort, Vermont

Some snowshoes are better at this than others. A back-country or mountain type of snowshoe features a suitable design, with reinforcements around the straps for aligning the boot and snowshoe to achieve maximum stability and control.

Walking downhill

Of course it's not necessary to sideslip or traverse down hills; in fact you want to avoid it, especially if the snow is hard. The sides of the snowshoes are tubular, so there's no way for them to grip firm snow. Sidestepping or traversing works on steeper slopes only if the snow is soft enough to make a dent.

Instead, walk straight down the hill, moving from heel to toe. Really dig your heel in, then your toe. If you try to go toe first, you'll slide. If it's really icy, push even harder so the claws or crampons dig in.

Breaking trail

When breaking new trails through fresh, and often deep, snow, it's best to use a snowshoe designed for the backcountry. These models are generally longer and wider to provide more stability in deep, heavy snow or buoyancy in light, fluffy snow.

Take small steps, moving from heel to toe (to prevent snow buildup in the front), while poling for rhythm and stability.

Top: When walking downhill, always move from heel to toe for the most stability. **Bottom:** Trekking through the woods and breaking your own trail is fun to do on snowshoes.

BUYING GEAR

As snowshoeing becomes more popular, the equipment gets more and more diversified and specialized. Snowshoes range from $100 to almost $400. The more expensive ones are made of lighter materials (such as carbon-graphite) and feature bindings that are easier to use or more sophisticated for technical applications.

There are carbon-graphite snowshoes for running, weighing less than two pounds and costing more than $300. There are hard-core backcountry snowshoes that have heavy-duty bindings and are sturdy enough for trudging in deep snow. And there are all-purpose snowshoes for cruising around basic terrain. Generally, snowshoes fall into the following categories:

Aerobic or fitness snowshoes are designed especially for running on the snow.

- **Aerobic or fitness.** Fitness-oriented snowshoes tend to be lighter, averaging from two to three pounds. The frames are designed to return more quickly for agile moves. Bindings are more suited for aerobic activity, providing more control and support for vigorous strides.

- **Recreational.** These basic, all-around snowshoes are the most reasonably priced. They're built on a medium-sized frame to provide good balance and stability. The bindings are user friendly and are designed to fit almost any size shoe; sometimes they feature heel plates to help center the foot. The materials used tend to be heavier than aerobic snowshoes but also are more resistant to wear and tear.

- **Hiking or climbing.** These bindings combine the features of fitness and backcountry snowshoes—they're light enough for endurance workouts but sturdy enough for heavy snow trekking. The bindings are designed to fit hiking boots and provide a secure fit so you don't wobble when doing tricky moves uphill.

- **Backcountry or adventure.** Backcountry shoes tend to have buckles instead of straps for easy maneuvering in foul weather. They have wide platforms for maximum buoyancy on the snow. They feature more aggressive crampons with powerful claws for gripping ice and slippery snow. The bindings are very sturdy for superior stability, and some brands feature special features like shaped footbeds. The frames are high quality so they're strong but not heavy; they're also designed to be durable in extreme conditions and temperatures.

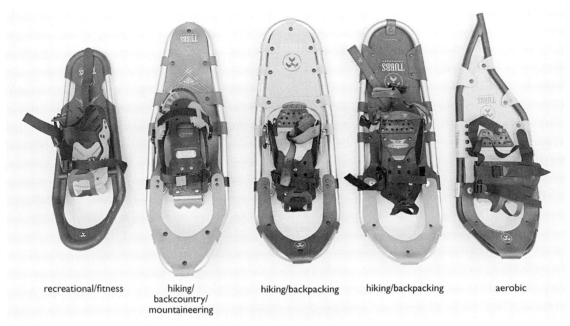

| recreational/fitness | hiking/
backcountry/
mountaineering | hiking/backpacking | hiking/backpacking | aerobic |

Modern snowshoes are designed for everything from hiking to aerobic exercise. The models shown are all especially designed for women.

More and more kids are enjoying snow-shoeing as manufacturers make especially designed snowshoes with appealing graphics and in fun shapes, such as animal paws.

- **Women's.** Women's snowshoes are relatively new, and the first companies to introduce them were Tubbs and Crescent Moon. They are designed to correspond to women's feet and our angle of walking. These snowshoes tend to be lighter and are shaped ergonomically (wide at the ball of the foot, narrow at the heel) for women's shorter strides. And the bindings on women's snowshoes are scaled to fit women's shoe sizes. "Women have a shorter, more lin-eally oriented stride," says Jake Thamm, presi-dent of Crescent Moon. You'll be able to find women's styles for most snowshoe activities.

- **Children's.** Kids' snowshoes range from $35 to $75. They're considerably smaller than adults' snowshoes. The bindings are designed to be easy to use even while wearing gloves or mittens. Some are miniversions of adults' snowshoes while others are lightweight polyurethane shaped like animals or pawprints.

ROUGHING IT OR NOT

Part of the fun of snowshoeing is to join in all the activities sprouting up at winter resorts or in your own hometown. From Vail's Snowshoe Shuffle, the biggest snowshoe race in the world, to the weekly nature hikes at the Trapp Family Lodge in Stowe, Vermont, it seems as if there's no end to the variety of options for snowshoers, whether new or seasoned.

Weekly moonlight tours organized by mountain resorts or Nordic centers are becoming more and more popular. Snowshoers typically wear headlamps and walk on gentle hiking terrain to a central point where someone has built a big bonfire and made hot chocolate. These are especially fun on moonlit nights when you don't even need the headlamps. Some country inns are organizing inn-to-inn guided snowshoe tours exploring local terrain off the beaten path. And snowshoe centers will cater to your every need or crazy whim, whether it's a group picnic tour, hiking combined with a gourmet meal, or a rugged backcountry overnight tour.

In Colorado, California, Montana, and other high-mountain locales there are hut-to-hut trips where you can snowshoe several miles a day and spend the night in huts along the way. It requires packing food, a sleeping bag, and extra clothing. Some people do it on their own, but it's best to use a guide.

If you prefer something remote yet lavish, there are lodges and cabins in the back of beyond that combine adventure with romance or luxurious amenities. Typically these places offer private cabins, with a central lodge for family-style eating. They may be so remote that you have to helicopter in (British Columbia has several).

So you see, taking up snowshoeing can offer a world of adventure or luxury (or both). You decide. See chapter 9 for specifics on adventure.

> "**S**nowshoeing is something you can do by yourself; you don't have to hire an instructor. I get the biggest kick when my students come back after their first lesson with me and say, 'Where should I go? I'm going snowshoeing today?' They come in, they rent their snowshoes, and they go up on a trail by themselves. They come in feeling independent and confident."
>
> —Patricia Hammon, instructor at Vail/Beaver Creek

Chapter 5

CROSS-COUNTRY SKIING

• •

The beauty of cross-country skiing is that it can be done practically anywhere—even in your own backyard.

• •

Nordic or cross-country skiing counts the most women among its fans of any snow-sliding sport—46 percent. It has a lot going for it. It's the least expensive, and it's getting even more affordable. It's also one of the best aerobic workouts and it's low impact, so you won't put strain on your joints.

Cross-country skiing dates back thousands of years, having its beginnings in Norway and other Scandinavian countries where skis were used to travel across the vast flat and snowy landscape. Ancient petroglyphs in Norway dating back to 2000 B.C. show figures on long skis using a single long pole to help them on their way. Even today, most Norwegians learn to ski almost as soon as they learn to walk. For kids it's just as common to use skis as sleds, and for adults cross-country skiing replaces jogging as the most popular wintertime exercise.

Yet in the United States cross-country skiing has gotten a bad rap over the years. Perhaps you believe some of the myths you've heard, such as "it's too much work" or, just the opposite, "if you can walk you can ski." Or maybe you've heard "it's boring and dull and only granola eaters do it." Well, if you meet a bunch of cross-country aficionados you'll change your thinking. These super athletes are in great shape and wear cool, colorful clothing that shows off their muscles.

In fact, cross-country skiing is a wonderful way to get out and enjoy winter, and it's really not hard to get started. There's a reason the sport was long promoted with the slogan "If you can walk, you can ski." It's easy to get the hang of it. But it has never become highly popular because it isn't really as easy as walking: it's quite a workout. But you're in control: you can make the workout as hard or as easy as you want it to be.

Don't approach the sport with the attitude that in no time you'll be cruising up and down hills and clocking the miles. It does take *some* effort to learn. Sadly, when they don't pick it up in a few minutes, many people get frustrated and quit. Listed in the sidebar are some of the concerns newcomers might have.

WHERE TO GO

But cross-country skiing is not all that difficult, either. And it's not necessary to take a lesson, although some instruction helps. Take Jackie Limroth, an athletic grandmother who likes to stay in shape. She tried the sport without having experience with any snow sports. For weeks before her trip, she practiced in her living room on a Nordic Track (an exercise machine that simulates cross-country skiing). And it paid off. Her first strides felt natural, and off she went, gliding along the trail. "I watched a video and practiced how I'd move my arms and legs so I'd have some idea what I had to do once I got the poles and skis on," she said.

• •

"Cross-country skiing is wonderful. You're just doing it for your own enjoyment. You don't have to be in an organized setting. And during big snowfalls when everyone else is stranded, I can just put on my backpack and go off to do the shopping on my cross-country skis. Cars aren't allowed, but I can go!"

—Deirdre Devlin, the author's mother

• •

COMMON CONCERNS

• • • • • • • • • • • • • • • • • •

- **Will I be too cold?** For cross-country skiing, you don't need heavy clothing. Because it's such an aerobic sport, participants may wear skimpy-looking outfits, yet they stay perfectly warm. The key is to dress in layers with pieces that are designed to wick away sweat so you stay dry. On colder days you should bundle up a little more, but not as much as with downhill skiing or snowboarding (see chapter 3, Staying Warm).

- **Do I have to ski down hills?** Eventually you'll want to ski down hills (that's part of what makes cross-country skiing fun), but in the beginning you can stick to flat areas. A golf course or a field is ideal for starting out. At cross-country ski areas there's always a flat beginner area to practice on. Once you go out on trails there are usually small hills, but there are special techniques for maneuvering down them (see pages 75–76 for more on hills).

(continued next page)

COMMON CONCERNS

• • • • • • • • • • • • • • • • • •

(continued from previous page)

- **If I fall off the track into deeper snow, how will I get up?** Typically, the snow off to the side is deeper than it is on the track, where it gets packed down from frequent use. If you fall into the deeper snow on the side, it's a little trickier to get up, but that's more because of stray branches and other obstacles than because of the snow itself. If you stick to the basic procedure for getting up after a fall and practice this so it becomes second nature, you'll find it becomes easy to get up almost anywhere (see page 75).

The beauty of cross-country skiing is that it can be done practically anywhere—even in your own backyard—once there's a snowfall. Even in New York City, people take to the streets when a big dump occurs. A local golf course, field, or bike trail is ideal. Make sure there's a minimum of two to three inches of snow. If you trek out on your own, you can rent cross-country skis at an outdoor shop or ski shop. Check ahead of time and find out who in your area rents gear so you'll know where to go when it does snow. Or invest in your own equipment so you'll have it when you need it (see pages 77–79).

If you want a more organized experience, you can visit a cross-country ski area, or touring center as they're generally called. Most mountain resorts also feature cross-country skiing, often on their golf courses. Some park districts or forest preserves maintain cross-country trails and rent equipment.

In the suburbs of New Jersey I often ski at a local bike trail. Even though there's nobody organizing trails, tracks form as people go out to enjoy the fresh snowfall. This is where I took my

Cross-country skiing can be done practically anywhere there's snow. Tamra Mooney, mother of three, goes out for a tour with her baby, Scott, on her back.

mother, Deirdre, for her first cross-country skiing experience, about ten years ago. It was great to drive five minutes and be somewhere we could enjoy the snow for free! My mother started on wider skis, which are ideal for beginners because they're more stable and feel less awkward. She also used sturdy boots that looked like hiking boots—they came up over her ankles.

The terrain on the bike trail was a bit tricky. Tracks from other skiers that had frozen overnight made it hard to keep the rhythm going. But soon we were gliding along side by side, not looking down to see if the skis fit in the tracks

Touring centers offer snowmaking, instruction, groomed trails, and guided tours.

but just enjoying the scenery and the conversation. That lumpy terrain was good practice, and when my mother later tried cross-country skiing on groomed tracks she was a natural.

Of course, setting out on the local golf course or bike trails is not as easy as skiing at an organized touring center where the tracks are groomed every day so you can just put your skis into them and follow. But it's close, convenient, and free, as well as being a good way to get a quick workout when you can't go off for the weekend.

My first Nordic experience was during college when a group of us decided to take an afternoon off from downhill skiing and teach ourselves cross-country. I loved it immediately, but what I appreciated most was the scenic setting. We went down a remote road and were soon in the middle of some fields, ready to start our adventure. We got the skis from a shack—no one was there. We fumbled our way into them and ventured off on that sunny day. With no idea what to wear, I had put on ski pants and a heavy jacket. Soon I was sweating profusely and had to shed layers. Tying the jacket around my waist proved cumbersome—but I was hardy, I was tough, and I kept going.

We did about four miles—quite a workout for a bunch of first-timers. But four miles on cross-country skis isn't as hard as it sounds—it's about the equivalent of jogging a mile when you're out of shape. It was so beautiful skiing along the winding trails through the woods, watching the sun peep through the trees and melt the ice on the branches, that I forgot how hard I was working to keep up with the fitness freaks ahead of me. It was so peaceful to be away from the bustle of the crowds at the ski resort.

A LESSON IN HUMILITY

• • • • • • • • • • • • • • • • • • •

Starr Ackley, 51, a professor of French at Albertson College in Idaho, is an enthusiastic cross-country skier who keeps in shape for her sport by regularly commuting to school on her bike (a fifty-mile round trip). She had been an avid downhill skier and took up Nordic skiing ten years ago after a knee injury. "I blew out my knee downhilling, and my doctor told me I wasn't strong enough yet for getting back on alpine skis. Once I tried it, I was hooked. Your own speed, your own ability level—no lifts, and you can really get out in the boonies. My most memorable experience? Feeling like hot stuff because I was doing the 30 K Boulder Mountain Tour for the first time at age 49. At the start, a woman who looked somewhat older than me asked if it was my first race, I replied proudly, 'Yes—and at 49!' 'How nice,' she said; 'you'll love it. I did my first race 15 years ago at 60 and have been coming here ever since.' What a role model! What a lesson in humility! That's what's so good about cross-country skiing—everyone gets equal respect regardless of level. The best are the most understated."

Not everyone gets to start off with the peace and privacy we had, but even the established touring centers can feel like this. Typically they're along a remote road or in some country setting. Some are very simple—perhaps an old-inn-turned-touring-center or just a shack with some rental skis. Others are more resortlike and feature a shop, an eating spot, and a separate rental area.

WHAT TO EXPECT AT A TOURING CENTER

Touring centers are often family-run, but even if they're not, the atmosphere is low-key and friendly. They may be in a golf course clubhouse, an old country inn, or a structure built for the purpose. All maintain a clublike atmosphere—a place where you can just hang out—and they always have someplace you can relax and eat a picnic lunch.

Typically you can expect to find rentals, lessons, and tickets for the trail network. The tickets can cost between $5 and $25 depending on how big the center is, how many trails it has, and how many amenities there are. The touring center maintains the trails, grooming them nightly, which really helps during iffy surface conditions. For example, a grooming machine can break up ice, making the surface less slippery. Some touring centers have snowmaking machines. Bigger trail networks will also have some sort of patrol skiing the trails to make sure visitors are all right and don't get lost. They'll always sweep the trails for stragglers at day's end. Many larger systems also have warming huts along the way. All touring centers have signs telling whether the trail is rated beginner, intermediate, or advanced. Most centers also provide maps.

When you arrive at a touring center, head to the information desk or ticket counter. Ask about specials combining ticket, lesson, and rental. Explore the building. You should find rest rooms, a cafeteria or lunchroom, a bulletin board with useful information including tips on where to go, notices of used gear for sale, and local activities and events (like moonlight tours), and a retail shop selling clothing, equipment, and accessories.

At bigger cross-country areas there are usually two sets of trails for the two main types of cross-country skiing, known as *diagonal stride* and *skating*. Skating is relatively new, and the motion looks a lot like ice-skating. The skating trails are flat and wide to accommodate the skaters' broader stride. For diagonal stride skiing, the more traditional form, the trails have two narrow tracks, one for each ski.

Many of my cross-country trips have been in remote areas with no organized trail system at all. On a trip to Jackson Hole, Wyoming, for example, I rented skis and boots at a local shop and headed off to Yellowstone National Park. What a wonderful opportunity to visit the famous park without competing with the summer crowds and worrying about stray grizzlies (since they hibernate in the winter)! A friend gave me a map and told me where I could explore. It was wide-open terrain surrounded by the beautiful Teton mountain range. For a while I skied along a small creek.

Skating on cross-country skis is the fastest way to go.

The sport of cross-country skiing really finds itself in atmospheres like Jackson, New Hampshire—a picturesque village with a covered bridge and many craft shops. Jackson revolves around Nordic skiing and is typical of the experience you can have on a cross-country ski vacation. The many inns and restaurants that cater to the ski crowd offer lunches and après-ski activities. The trails themselves are beautiful, through the woods, next to frozen creeks, across open fields. One trail ends up at an inn where after five miles of vigorous skiing you're ready for the hot soup, hot chocolate, and sandwiches sold here.

TECHNIQUES

For such a simple sport, cross-country skiing can seem complicated because there are so many varieties. The sport and its equipment can be divided into three categories: recreational, performance, and telemarking.

Cross-country ski anatomy: tip (front), waist (middle, with binding), and tail (end). Camber is the vertical bow of the ski in the grip zone.

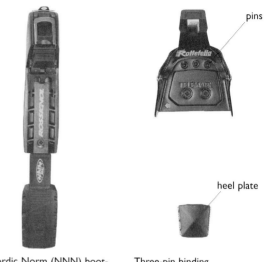

pins

heel plate

New Nordic Norm (NNN) boot-binding system

Three-pin binding

Right and below: Bindings are largely a matter of preference, but the binding system on your skis must match the binding system on your boots. **Three-pin bindings** have three small pins that fit into three small holes on the front of the boot (below, 1). Most skiers, however, use boot-binding systems with a bar on the boot toe that clicks into an opening on the binding (below, 2–5).

Recreational skiing, also called *touring* or *classic skiing*, consists of the traditional *kick and glide* or *diagonal stride*. This motion follows the natural strides of running or jogging—with arms and legs moving opposite each other. It's the easiest technique to learn. Skis can be either traditional (long and skinny) or midlength (shorter and wider). Of late the shorter, wider models have been popular for beginners. They're easier to maneuver and provide more stability.

Performance skiing covers racing, skate skiing, or high-energy classic skiing. *Skating* was developed by racers in order to go faster. Now an entire category has evolved. While the motion looks a lot like skating on skates, skiers push the edges of the skis against the snow. *High-energy classic* or *fitness skiing* is for those who want to ski fast and hard to get an intense workout in a short time. Equipment for fitness skiing is lighter and higher performing.

Telemark skiing is a technique for going downhill. It started as a backcountry skill and has slowly become more mainstream. It includes that graceful move where the skier drops a knee to carve a turn down the mountain. The equipment can be similar to downhill ski equipment, but it's often lighter, and the bindings are more like cross-country bindings where the heel is free. Some telemark bindings use a cable mechanism that can lock the heel down if needed. Most telemark skis for lift-assisted skiing have metal edges.

THE BASICS

Although it's quite possible to learn some of the basic moves on the NordicTrack as Jackie Limroth did (see page 65), taking a lesson is recommended. I've taken many lessons over the years and found there's a lot more to the sport than I originally thought. Picking up tips from pros helped make my stride more efficient so I could ski faster with less effort. Cross-country skiing looks so easy that it's amazing to ski behind someone who is better than you and find that even though you think you're doing the same thing, soon that person is far ahead of you.

When you're not taking a lesson, though, there are many basic skills you can practice on your own. Learn these skills and practice the drills, and you'll improve much faster as you begin to feel comfortable with long boards on your feet. Many of the skills you learn in lessons are useful in more advanced skiing situations. To get a lesson, you'll need to find a cross-country or touring center. During the first lesson you'll learn how to put the skis on, how to glide, how to stop, and how to turn on your skis.

Be sure to wear proper clothing. For cross-country skiing this means layers: long underwear (wear a fabric that wicks moisture away from the skin—not cotton), fleece top, stretchy Lycra-type warm-up pants, and a lightweight wind shell. If it's really cold you'll want to wear more—perhaps adding a down vest or substituting a heavier shell. If it's warmer, just the fleece top should suffice. You may want to wear gaiters to keep snow out of your boots. See chapter 3 for more details on apparel.

There are many choices in cross-country equipment (see pages 78–79 for more specifics). When starting out, it's best to rent gear. You'll be given no-wax touring skis appropriate for skiing in tracks. If you want to skate, which is harder to learn, you'll have to ask for skating equipment.

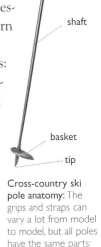

Cross-country ski pole anatomy: The grips and straps can vary a lot from model to model, but all poles have the same parts: grip, strap, shaft, basket, and tip.

Putting on the gear

Choose a flat area that's not icy, with plenty of room around you. Once the skis are on you'll be getting ready to move out, and you don't want to encounter a hill right away. Even a little incline can be scary when just starting out, especially if you've never had much experience with snow or felt your feet slide. If there are hills around you, carry your gear and walk down to a flat area. Be careful, because the boots sometimes have slippery soles—stay to the side and look for soft snow that you can dig your feet into.

Getting the skis on can be a bit tricky, but it's gotten easier. There are two basic types of bindings: more modern step-in systems or the old-fashioned three-pin system. The newer ones are designed so you can lock the boots into the bindings while standing up; typically there's a metal slot or bar on the toe of the boot that clicks into the binding. The idea is that you just need to line your toe up with the binding and step down until you hear a click. The old-

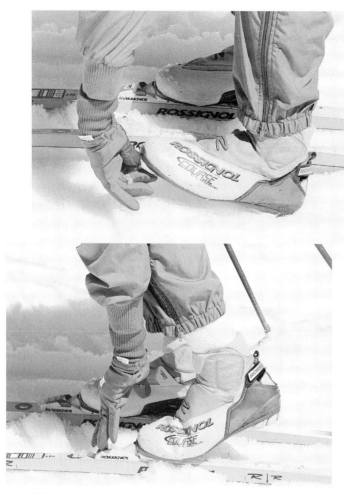

When putting on your cross-country skis, first clear out all the snow from the sole and toe area (top). Then line up the toe of your boot with the front of the binding and click in (bottom).

fashioned three-pin system is harder to use; you have to line up three holes in the toe of the boot with three pins on the binding and then bend down to clamp a lever over the toe area. There's no right or left ski, so it doesn't matter which one goes on which foot. Once you're latched in, balance evenly on both feet with the ski poles planted in the snow at your sides.

The main secret in fastening either sort of binding is to make sure the boot sole is clear of snow or ice, including the toe area where the binding attaches. If a lot of snow has gotten in, you'll have to use your fingers—sometimes with gloves on, sometimes not, depending on how easily the snow comes off.

To grasp the poles properly, slide your hands up through the straps from the bottom and grip straps and poles together.

Practice in place

Before leaving your flat area, try to get the feel of those long boards without moving too far. This can also be a good way to warm up. Practice lifting one foot, then the other. You can use your poles for balance; keep them outside your skis, slightly in front of your feet, with your arms bent at a ninety-degree angle. If you're finding it easy to balance, try lifting one foot without using your poles. Then jump up and down in place. Next, keeping both skis firmly on the ground, glide forward on one foot and then the other. Try taking baby steps forward, barely lifting one ski at a time.

Turning in place

As you get comfortable taking your baby steps, start to angle your skis to turn around. Move the tails apart in a wedge shape, then bring them back together, one step at a time—first the right ski, then the left, always turning until you're facing the opposite way. Make sure you're using little steps—there's no need to rush. If you take bigger steps you may cross your tips and get tangled up or fall. Just be patient. Once you're comfortable you can try bigger steps. Small steps continue to be handy for turning in tight spaces, though, such as at the top of a mountain where there's not much room to maneuver.

The grip and poling

Poling rhythm in cross-country skiing is as natural as walking. First practice without skis, planting one pole forward as the leg on that side goes back. Poles also help you balance and can even hold you up a bit as you try to get stable and establish your stride.

The grip on cross-country poles is important, much more so than in alpine skiing. The upper body plays a key role, and learning to pole properly is essential. That starts with your grasp. The pole strap should be fairly snug around your hand, positioned underneath it so that you're pushing down more on the strap than on the pole grip itself. As you push off, be sure to follow through all the way until your hand is behind your thigh.

The pole strap should fit snugly around your hand. This particular pole has a **glove strap**.

To start the pole plant, reach well out in front, pushing down on the grip, and keep pushing until you're well ahead of the pole. Then release your grasp as you start to plant the opposite pole.

Follow through all the way back with your arms when you're **double poling**.

Sliding, gliding, and double poling

Continue to work on the exercises described on page 72 in a flat area. Gliding on flat terrain will give you confidence when you begin sliding down an incline. It's important to get comfortable with the sensation of sliding, especially if you've never felt it before.

To start, take note of your stance—the way you stand on your skis. Your arms should be in front of your body, your knees should be bent, and your upper body should be centered over the skis.

A good exercise to get the feel of gliding and balancing is to slide on one foot—just like riding a scooter. Take one ski off and use your free foot to push while the ski glides along.

Now try gliding with both skis. To thrust your body forward and get a burst of momentum, you'll need

to *double pole*. Position both poles in front of you, bend your knees, and lower your hips as you push both poles downward into the snow, driving them backward to propel your body forward. Your arms should extend all the way back before you bring them forward for another go. Do two or three double-pole strokes and then relax in your stance—just let your skis glide along. Double poling is also an excellent technique for giving your legs a rest out on the trail, since your arms do all the work.

Edging or sidestepping

Most cross-country skis do not have metal edges like alpine skis (the exceptions being telemark and some heavy-duty touring skis; see below on gear), and therefore they don't dig into the snow as much. But the technique for going uphill is basically the same as with alpine skiing. Start with both skis parallel (across the hill) and begin to step sideways up the hill. Push the outside edge of the uphill ski into the snow so it feels firmly planted, then do the same with the other ski, bringing both skis parallel again. Keep doing this until you've made it up the hill. Sidestepping is also a handy way to get down a hill when you don't feel you can handle steep terrain.

Herringbone

A lot of the moves in cross-country skiing are similar to alpine skiing, but Nordic skis are lighter, and having your heel free lends more mobility. The *herringbone* entails climbing uphill using the inner edges of your skis. Picture your skis moving uphill in a V shape, making a pattern like herringbone tweed. Starting at the bottom, spread your ski tips apart and start making steps first with one ski and then with the other, maintaining the V shape. As you step forward, press on the inside edges of the skis so they grip the snow firmly. Plant your poles alternately.

This is an important maneuver for going uphill. When hills are too long or too steep, it's

Top: Keep your skis parallel while sidestepping up the hill.
Bottom: As you herringbone up the hill, press on the inside edges of the skis so they grip the snow.

hard to get up them with the normal diagonal stride. That's when you shift to the herringbone.

Kick

The kick is the key move in the traditional diagonal stride. It's usually taught in intermediate lessons. Simply put, it's the motion of pushing (kicking) downward on the ski so it will grip the snow, then spring back and go forward. The center of the ski flexes in an upward bend, or *camber*, and if you position your body correctly, your weight will flatten out the bend so the center of the ski grips the snow to push you along. It's a beautiful feeling of rhythm and flow—one leg and then the other kicking as you glide.

As you kick, it's important to have your body weight forward and moving toward the front of your foot to help thrust you ahead. Sometimes women don't realize they're too far

The classic **diagonal stride** (which really means your opposite arm moves with each leg) requires a kick-and-glide motion, pushing down to flatten the camber so the ski grips the snow and pushing back for momentum (skier's left leg is finishing the kick; right leg is gliding forward).

back on their skis. Because we have a lower center of mass (with more weight below), we have to be especially conscious about keeping our weight forward—at least in the beginning.

Getting up from a fall

Falling down on cross-country skis is not serious because they're so lightweight, but you may find yourself tangled up. First, straighten yourself out by getting your skis parallel and on the downhill side and putting your poles in front of you. (You may have to roll onto your back and swing your skis overhead.) Make sure your skis are pointed across any incline so they won't slide. Pull your feet back under you, move forward onto your knees, and dig your poles into the snow so you can use your arms to push yourself up. It's considerably easier to do this on cross-country skis than on alpine skis, since your heels aren't fastened down. If worse comes to worst, you can take one ski off.

Wedging and braking

The *wedge* is like what used to be called the snowplow in alpine skiing; your skis form a V as you move down the hill with your ski tips together. By pushing both heels out to the sides, you achieve a braking effect.

Start out on a flat area and stand with your feet apart. Practice pushing the tails of the skis outward. Then find a gentle incline and, as you start to pick up speed, push the tails out to the sides while tilting the skis inward to engage their edges. This helps you slow down. The more you

GOING DOWNHILL: IT'S NOT AS HARD AS IT LOOKS

Certainly one of the most intimidating aspects of cross-country skiing is going down the hills, which is harder than on alpine skis because there are no edges to dig in and your heels are free, making it harder to turn the skis.

Kim Bender, a cross-country ski instructor for Vail Resorts in Colorado, has a unique way of getting her female students to ski downhill comfortably. She says, "I like to keep the fun in the fundamentals." For each skill she teaches, she has an amusing analogy that helps women relate to the sport more quickly. "In order to enjoy the trail system around the Rocky Mountains," she explains, "you've got to have some hill skills. It's real easy to go up them, but coming down you need some good technique so you don't hurt yourself." But hills aren't found only in the Rockies. Most cross-country centers around the country have plenty, even on beginner trails.

Kim uses the second half of a beginner lesson to teach the wedge and its dynamics. She starts teaching hill skills on the flats. "It's like flight school: you do lots and lots of ground school before you get to fly." The wedge requires pushing both heels out to the sides as you move down the hill. The first exercise Kim teaches toward achieving the wedge is double poling, standing wide on both skis, and simply pushing the tails outward. "If they don't have a concept of the edging that has to happen with the wedge, I'll back up a notch." She tells her students to stand still and make the biggest pile of snow they can (like making snow angels) by moving their legs outward from the hip and the heel so the skis push up the snow. "I really swing my hip out there— women can relate to the hip thing. You have to tilt your edges. It's like spreading frosting on a cake—if you tilt the knife too far it will dig in and wreck the cake. If you tilt it just right the frosting will spread beautifully. Basically you want to use the inside edge of your skis to spread that frosting from the hip and from the heel."

Bender says that as her students glide and spread out their skis they learn about pressure and edging. Once they get comfortable, she has them try bigger glides, with a little more speed and a bigger wedge.

tilt the skis the more the edges will dig into the snow, until you stop altogether. (See sidebar above for more tips on wedging.)

If you are a novice, wedge turns work best for downhills and corners. More advanced skiers can use a *skate turn* for corners, which requires quickly transferring weight from one ski to the next. A *wedge christy turn* combines the wedge with a skidded parallel turn. The *telemark turn* uses a bent knee to carve a turn. But unless you're planning to go downhill a lot, you won't need to learn these turns.

Use the **wedge** to curb your speed going down hills.

MORE ADVANCED SKIING: SKATING AND BACKCOUNTRY

Beyond these basics, the best way to improve is to take lessons. Kicking is best learned by skiing behind an instructor or a skier who knows how to do it. Once you understand the basic principles behind the technique, seeing it done really helps.

Skating is another advanced technique, popular in racing. It's really not that difficult, especially if you've done ice-skating or in-line skating. It's done on a flat surface with no tracks, so it can be ideal if you're on a golf course or in a field that doesn't have tracks laid anyway. Skating requires timing, power, and grace. To start, push off on your left ski with a double poling action—poles out in front thrusting backward to power you forward. As your arms go back, the right foot steps forward, ready to repeat the maneuver, waiting for your arms to come forward again.

As you progress in the sport, you may decide to enter races or get into fitness training. There are many cross-country races to join, and these can give you an adrenaline rush and a reason to stay in shape during the winter. You may just enjoy "touring," logging miles as you wander through beautiful, peaceful scenery. Or maybe you're the adventurous type and want to explore remote territory, charting new backcountry terrain in the mountains. Many people learn cross-country skiing so they can telemark, which is easier when you have a combination of alpine and cross-country skills. See chapter 9, Resources, for information on where to go backcountry skiing.

BUYING GEAR

Where to buy

Before you buy, spend some time renting equipment or trying demo (demonstration) gear. This will help you to decide whether you really like cross-country skiing and what type you want to do. Who knows? You may consider yourself an inactive person only to find you're racing through the forest, wanting to go faster and faster.

You can rent gear at the touring center or at a local cross-country or outdoor shop. Expect to pay anywhere from $10 to $25 for a day. A larger touring center that offers a wide variety of equipment in the latest models will be on the high side; a smaller outfit will be cheaper.

When it comes time to buy, be aware that it's very difficult to buy cross-country gear through ski swaps, garage sales, or newspaper ads. A reliable Nordic shop is one place to look for used gear, however. The reason it's not wise to buy used gear is that so much of it has become obsolete. You might pay $50 for a set of skis only to find that the bindings are no longer being made, so you won't be able to find boots to fit them. New bindings cost about $30 to $60, and new boots may run $50 to $150. If you do buy used gear, be sure to get skis, boots, and bindings all at once.

It's often cheaper to buy a ski package, which offers all the components at a discount. Prices can range from $200 to $600, but most recreational ski packages, with skis, bindings, boots, and poles, will range between $200 and $400. One of the least expensive ways to buy cross-country skis is through catalogs from national outdoor companies like L.L. Bean, REI, and Eastern Mountain Sports (EMS). These catalogs typically offer inexpensive packages from well-known brands like Karhu and Salomon. But it's also nice to visit a Nordic shop that has qualified sales help who can steer you to the right selection

What to buy

Not so long ago, buying a pair of cross-country skis was simple. "Reach up as far as you can," a salesperson would say (skis were measured by the distance to your wrist; now weight is the main consideration rather than height). And voilà, skis and length were chosen all at once. Times have changed. The beautiful wooden cross-country skis of yesteryear became a thing of the past when lighter, fiberglass skis with wood cores took over.

Now there are many types of cross-country skis, and what to buy will be determined by the type of skiing you plan to do. What length to choose can also be confusing. A shop salesperson or your instructor can help you determine the proper size. In the 1990s, new, midlength touring skis were introduced. These skis, much shorter than traditional skis, were designed to make skiing easier for first-timers. They're more size-appropriate for women and are an excellent choice for starting out.

Midlength skis are typically no-wax, which means they have a machined pattern on the bottom, or base, to help the ski grip the snow so you don't have to apply the appropriate kicker wax each time. They're also more versatile, and one ski can work for skiing in-track or out-of-track (breaking your own trail through the woods or on a golf course). Because they're wider, the skis break through new snow more easily. The downside is that they don't glide as easily as more traditionally designed skis. Waxable cross-country skis are recommended if you plan to pursue the sport seriously. There are many different types of waxes for different ranges of temperatures (hard waxes are for colder days; soft waxes for warmer days). The art of waxing skis properly is a lifelong practice. But, a ski waxed right offers superior performance.

Traditional cross-country skis are long and skinny. High-performance models, for racing or fitness skiing, are lighter and typically have waxable bases. Some skis also have metal edges on the forebody or front part of the ski for more control going downhill. These skis also can have varying degrees of flex, or camber, which you need to choose. One ski might come in two cambers, designed to suit a person's weight and ability level. A stiffer-flexing ski requires more energy and power to kick.

Traditionally designed skis for recreational skiing or touring look similar to the performance or racing models, but they weigh more and generally have no-wax bases.

Skating skis are shorter and waxable, geared toward skiers who want to race or get a high-level workout. They're generally more expensive, but the construction is ultra-lightweight and you get a choice of camber.

Telemark skis are a cross between alpine and cross-country skis. Like alpine skis, they're heavier to provide more stability when you're going fast, and they have metal edges to hold on ice for downhill skiing. The construction is also more torsionally rigid, which makes the skis harder to turn but provides better grip on ice. Like cross-country touring skis they use a free-heel binding, though it may be possible to lock the heel down.

There are no specific women's designs in cross-country skis, but women's boots are undergoing great innovations. When choosing a boot, look for one that has a last specifically formed to fit a woman's foot and accommodate the lower foot volume, narrower heel, and higher instep. The latest styles also feature self-molding foams that conform to different foot shapes. Often women's boots will also have extra insulation; look for Thinsulate and fleece linings. Some boots may have wider openings to fit women's calves and other special features to fit the typical woman. They come in varying cuff heights: shorter styles are for racing or fitness skiing, whereas over-the-ankle cuts are for touring and backcountry treks.

Be aware that boots are designed to fit specific types of bindings: you cannot mix and match. it's best to buy the two together so you don't end up with bindings that don't fit your boots.

Nordic bindings have come a long way in the past couple of decades. The older style of

Cross-country skiing is easier at a touring center where ski tracks are well defined and easy to maneuver through.

binding for cross-country is known as the three-pin or 75 millimeter, and this design is still used for telemark skiing (see photos page 70). For recreational touring or fitness skiing, newer, step-in binding systems have been developed that are far more efficient and much easier to click in and out of (see photos page 70). The most common brands are Salomon's SNS system and Rottefella's NNN system (for New Nordic Norm); several boot brands are designed to fit these bindings. The best boot-binding systems are designed to keep snow out of the binding opening so you don't have to reach down to clear it with your fingers. Bindings are sold separately from boots and skis; they need to be mounted (drilled) onto the skis by a technician.

Cross-country poles are usually made of lightweight fiberglass (see photo page 71). Racers and serious skiers generally choose a more high-tech model made of carbon-graphite for strength and lightness. Poles should be at shoulder height or slightly higher if you're planning to skate.

Chapter 6

DOWNHILL SKIING

Former U.S. Ski Team member Vicki Fleckenstein-Woodworth blasts down the slopes of Okemo Mountain in southern Vermont.

THE ADVENTUROUS WINTER SPORT

Although the Norwegians probably made the first "official" downhill ski turns, alpine or downhill skiing got its real start in the Alps when the Austrians started experimenting with turns. In the late 1800s Mathias Zdarsky found that a crouching turn (which eventually evolved into the snowplow) could get him down some steep hills. By the 1920s ski schools opened in Austria, and the sport came to the United States soon afterward.

Women have been skiing since the early days, when they did it in long skirts! Though social conditions have improved, downhill skiing is still probably the most intimidating of all of the snow sports to women—or at least it was until snowboarding came along and replaced it. And, although it looks scary to women, skiing is also intriguing. Perhaps that's partly because skiing has always been perceived as the sport of the rich

● ●

"I think what I always liked about skiing is that it's a personal challenge. I like sports where I compete with myself. I liked the speed of downhill skiing, and as scared as it made me, I loved how I felt when I made it down—strong, powerful, and capable. I loved using my muscles, being sore and tired yet exhilarated at the end of the day."

—Mary Robinson, grant writer

● ●

and famous, which certainly adds to the "cool" factor. We've all seen footage of Jacqueline Kennedy Onassis and Princess Diana enjoying the Alps with their children. We've heard about Oprah Winfrey's house in picturesque Telluride, Colorado, and we've all seen shots of Christie Brinkley and Cindy Crawford on the slopes.

Yet the sad truth is that many women are afraid to try skiing. I've seen many women sitting in the ski lodge reading or just hanging out while Dad and the kids are enjoying invigorating downhill runs in the cold winter air. Why do so many avoid it? Often their first experiences were not good ones. It's no wonder some women give up. At Snowbird in Utah a couple of years ago, I saw a woman flat on her back on the beginner hill, struggling to get up. Her husband was a few feet farther down the hill. "Am I going to have to walk up there and get you?" he bellowed. She looked helpless and, no doubt, was embarrassed, with onlookers from the chairlift watching the whole scene.

CONQUER THE CHALLENGE

Despite all the fears you might have about skiing, it's easy to get hooked. And rest assured that even the world's best skiers have experienced tough times at some point. The challenge is partly what makes skiing fun: once you overcome a barrier you feel invincible—not only on the slopes, but in your everyday life. That's what my friend Mary Robinson likes about skiing. "I think what I always liked about skiing is that it's a personal challenge. I like sports where I compete with myself. I liked the speed of

COMMON CONCERNS

● ● ● ● ● ● ● ● ● ● ● ● ● ● ● ● ● ●

- **How will I get off the chairlift?** Just riding the lift intimidates many new skiers, and getting off is even more frightening. Yet it really isn't that bad. Your first ride will undoubtedly be on a beginner chair. These travel slowly, and the lift attendants are trained to help you on and watch while you ski off. If there are any problems, the attendant will stop the lift and assist you. (See pages 89–90 on how to ride a chairlift.)

- **I'm afraid I'll go too fast and won't be able to stop.** This is a perfectly normal fear. But once you learn to snowplow in your very first ski lesson, you'll gain confidence. You'll see that you can slow down when you want or come to a complete stop by doing a snowplow using the metal edges on your skis.

(continued next page)

(continued from previous page)

- **Skiing is too expensive.** It's true that lift tickets at some resorts can be as high as $60 for a day of skiing. But the average price is between $35 and $45, and at some resorts you can ski for as little as $20 a day (if you go midweek). The key is to choose a smaller ski area that is not well known. This is where you'll find the bargains—on lift tickets, food, and other things. If you're just starting out, ask about a beginner package that offers a lift ticket, a lesson, and equipment rental at a special rate. Resorts also offer discounts on lift tickets if you ski more than one day, and you can sometimes buy discounted tickets at places like ski shops, supermarkets, and gas stations.

COMMON CONCERNS

downhill skiing, and as scared as it made me, I loved how I felt when I made it down—strong, powerful, and capable. I loved using my muscles, being sore and tired, yet exhilarated at the end of the day."

I still remember my first ride up on a chairlift, at age 13. I found it truly frightening. After a lesson and some practice, my best friend Kathy and I had graduated from the rope tow, and we were ready for the big slopes at Great Gorge, New Jersey (now called Mountain Creek). Once on the lift, we had to pull the safety bar down quickly as we were whizzing up a steep pitch over a small pond. Kathy was too nervous to do it, so I went for it but lost my poles.

Then I panicked. How would I manage without my poles? "Maybe our instructor will give me his," I said to Kathy. But he didn't, and I was quite upset about that. Of course years later I realized his poles would have been too long for me anyway. It seems like common sense now, but it was hard to think straight while trying to negotiate icy slopes on a bitter cold, windy night.

No matter, one shaky experience did not deter me. I loved skiing. I loved the sense of accomplishment, especially after skiing down without poles—I thought it was such a big deal. I loved the freedom and elation. I still do! It makes me feel alive, and when I'm skiing I can't think of anything else.

ARRIVING AT THE RESORT

When you go a ski resort for the first time, don't head straight for the rental shop to pick out skis or to the ticket window to buy a lift ticket. And don't let a friend talk you into letting him or her teach you (unless that person has had teaching experience at a resort).

The first thing you should do is sign up for a "learn to ski" package, which typically includes a lesson, equipment rental, and lift ticket. Prices can range from $20 to $55. If you're in Aspen, you'll pay top dollar, but at a smaller resort you're more likely to pay in the $20 to $30 range. A small resort is a good place to begin, and it can be less intimidating than the mega areas. Inquire at the ticket window about these packages and the attendant should be able to help you or point you in the right direction.

Many ski resorts also conduct women's ski clinics. Typically these sessions will provide female-friendly instruction and education about the challenges a woman faces in skiing. Some clinics also include sessions before and after skiing that cover stretching and yoga. Others may bring in a sports psychologist to address fears or a physical therapist to discuss injuries. For more on women's clinics, read the sidebar on Jeannie Thoren in this chapter (page 92) and check out the resource guide in chapter 9.

RENTING GEAR

The rental shop scene can be a bit crazy, so give yourself plenty of time before the lesson to get geared up. You'll be asked to fill out a form, and you'll have to wait in various lines to get your boots, skis, and poles. Some rental shop employees are more friendly and helpful than others; don't let a condescending smart kid intimidate you into rushing. Remember, they were once first-timers too.

Take your time finding boots that feel right. Be sure to ask for women's boots. Ideally, you'll be wearing ski socks (not cotton) that aren't too thick. Your socks should be pulled up tight and smooth so there are no wrinkles to cause discomfort.

Ask a shop employee to show you how to put the boots on. You need to unbuckle them and slide your feet in toe first. Stamp down on your heels to make sure you're completely in before buckling up. Don't try to fasten the boots too tight. The first notch on the buckle is plenty to determine if the boots fit OK. Do they feel snug without cutting off your circulation? Boots that are too tight will make your feet colder. How should a proper fit feel? Your heel shouldn't lift up, and you should be able to wiggle your toes. Don't be shy about trying on several sizes or styles to find the right fit.

After you find the right boots, go to the ski counter. Take off one of your boots and give it to the attendant, who will find skis that are the right size for you and adjust the bindings to your boot size. Most rental shops are now giving beginners "shaped" skis that are shorter than the earlier straight versions (see pages 93–94). Lengths typically range from 130 to 170 centimeters, depending on your height. Shorter skis are easier to turn, so start with supershort beginner skis if the rental shop has them.

Last but not least, you'll get a pair of ski poles. To determine if they're the right size, turn one upside down and grip it underneath the plastic basket. Your forearm should be at a right angle to the pole. Poles for downhill skiing have the same parts as cross-country poles—grip, strap, shaft, basket, and tip—although styles are different.

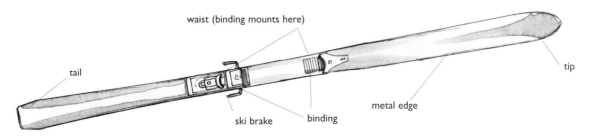

Alpine ski anatomy: tip (front), waist (middle), and tail (end). Bindings are placed in the middle, with binding toe toward the ski tip and binding heel toward the tail. Ski brakes attach to the binding heel.

Now you're almost ready to go. But first find a locker where you can leave your street shoes or boots before you try to walk outside with all your ski gear. Sometimes there are lockers downstairs from the rental shop; some shops also let you leave shoes under benches or in cubbyholes. It can be overwhelming trying to keep track of everything. Be sure you have a zipped pocket for your wallet and car keys. (See chapter 3 for information on what to wear.)

When you leave carrying your gear, be careful. Hold the poles in one hand and skis in the other. Keep the skis together by using the *ski brakes*—prongs attached to the binding, meant to stop runaway skis after a fall. When you place the ski bottoms together, the brakes jut out and can be interlocked. Grip your skis below the bindings and carry them with the tips pointing up. Always hold ski poles with tips down. If it's not crowded and you feel strong, you can put the skis over your shoulder with tips facing down. But this is a bit hard to do, and you have to be careful not to whack anyone in the face.

Always walk heel to toe in your ski boots and try to stay balanced. By taking slow, deliberate steps you should be able to make your way to the learning area where you'll begin your lesson. If it's icy or slippery, try to walk near a fence or something you can hold on to for extra stability.

If during your first few hours on the slopes you feel the equipment is not right for you, take it back to the rental shop. You can exchange boots, skis, or poles at any time. Ask your instructor for help if you're not sure. (See chapter 3 and the gear section beginning on page 91 for more specifics on skis and boots.)

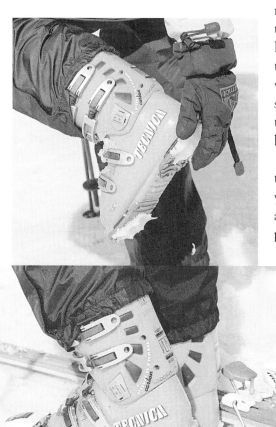

Before putting on your skis, clean the snow off the bottom of your boot (top). Then line up the toe of your boot with the toe piece of the binding. Make sure the heel is lined up and the boot is straight before stepping down to click in (bottom).

THE BASICS

Putting skis on and moving on flat terrain

Although you'll most likely have an instructor teaching you the basics, it's a good idea to get familiar with your equipment by doing a few exercises. If you can master these steps, you'll be well on your way to becoming a skier. You can even practice some of them in

The safest way to stand on the hill is with your skis parallel to each other and horizontal to the hill. Consider this home base. It's the best way to put skis on, and it's the best way to begin climbing a hill.

Make sure your stance is correct: hands in front with upper body slightly forward and knees and hips flexed.

your living room, without all the distractions of snow, weather, people, and slopes.

Before you can ski, you have to learn to walk and feel comfortable wearing your skis. To put your skis on, place them side by side perpendicular to the slope—that is, not facing down the hill even if you're on what looks like a flat spot. There is no left or right ski. Put your hands through the pole straps and hold the plastic part (grip) of the pole firmly. Push the poles into the snow one on each side of the skis just in front of the bindings. Holding on to your poles, lift one foot and line it up over the binding, toe first. Put your foot on the ski and push down on the heel until you hear the binding click into place. Then do the same with the other foot. You may have to use your hand or your pole to clean the snow off the bottom of your boots before you can click in. To release the bindings, use the tip of your pole to push down on the heel part of the binding. Always do one ski at a time and make sure one foot is on the ground before you try to get out of the other ski. Practice getting in and out of your bindings.

Now try to get comfortable on your skis while standing in one place. Slide one ski forward and back and then try to slide them back and forth alternately in rhythm while maintaining your balance. Try lifting one ski and then the other. Make some very small jumps in place. Stretch down, bending your knees. Doing all this while maintaining your balance will make you feel more relaxed on your skis, which can seem very awkward and clunky at first.

While practicing your moves, pay attention to your *stance*—the way you're standing on the skis. Your skis should be hip-width apart, your knees and hips flexed, and your upper body positioned slightly forward. Don't exaggerate this by bending at the waist, and don't stick out your derriere. Try to relax.

Next, walk forward on the flat terrain. Start very slowly with baby steps, barely lifting your skis off the ground. As you move your left leg, your right arm should also move forward in a steady rhythm. Go around in a circle to get the feeling of the motion. Also practice moving from side to side. Lift one ski and move it away from the other, then bring the other one next to it.

Congratulations! If you can do all these exercises and moves without crossing your skis or getting tangled up, you're already on your way to becoming a skier.

Baby steps to turn

After you've mastered some of the exercises above, you can try turning around on your skis, continuing to take baby steps. Turning around on the flats is easy if you take your time. And, it helps with balance and coordination. Begin with both skis parallel and across the *fall line* (the most direct path down the mountain). Take the top ski (the one closest to the top of the hill) and move it forward (about four inches), pointing it slightly in the direction of downhill (so you're starting the turn). Now bring the other ski right next to the first one. Keep doing this while continuing to turn the lead ski slightly. Always take baby steps! If you try to move too fast you may cross your tips and fall. It may seem tedious, but eventually you'll feel more coordinated and can do this faster. As you make your baby steps, try sliding the skis instead of lifting them.

Gliding with a pole push

Once you've completed the turn, practice gliding by using a *pole push*. Stand in a parallel position across the hill. Be aware of your stance—knees bent, upper body slightly forward. Push on your poles and slide forward, keeping both skis parallel. Notice how it feels to glide along. Push harder to go a bit faster.

Put pressure on your uphill edges when **sidestepping** up the hill so you don't slip down.

Edging and sidestepping

Now that you know how it feels to slide, it's time to try *edging*. Edging means putting pressure on the sides of your skis so the metal edges do what they're supposed to do—dig in and grip the snow.

When you're ready to practice sidestepping up the mountain by edging, you must stand with your skis parallel to each other and horizontal to the hill. Consider this home base. It's the best way to put skis on, and it's the best way to begin climbing a hill. Lift the uphill ski (the one closest to the top) and take a small step sideways to move it up the hill. Bring the downhill ski up next to it. As you sidestep up the hill, tip your skis so that the uphill edges push sideways into the hill. If your skis stayed flat on the snow you might slide down the hill.

Herringbone

The *herringbone* works for both alpine skiing and cross-country skiing (see pages 74–75). Think of placing your skis in a V shape, like the pattern in herringbone tweed, with tips pointing outward two to three feet apart, facing up the hill. This is how you'll walk up the hill. You must also use your edges, rolling your ankles and knees inward and angling your skis so both inside edges press into the hill. Take exaggerated, deliberate steps as you walk straight up the hill.

For balance, plant the pointed end of the pole in the snow on the outside of the ski. Make one pole plant at a time, on the same side you step on for balance.

Uh-oh. Now you've herringboned up but you don't know how to turn on the hill. You don't have to ski down yet. You can just practice sidestepping again going down. Sidestepping is useful even when you're an advanced skier, because it can help you out of tight spots like a very narrow patch of snow between some trees. Dig the upper edge of the downhill ski in first and then follow with the uphill ski.

When you fall

To get up from a fall, try to get back into the parallel position with skis together, pointed across the hill, with the uphill edges digging into the snow. Plant your poles together, on the uphill side of your body, and use them to push yourself up. You can also take your skis off by reaching back and pushing down on the heel part of your binding. Free one boot at a time. Once you've taken your skis off you can place them parallel across the hill, facing in the direction you want to go, and put them on again just as you did down by the base lodge.

To get up from a fall, plant your poles (1) so they're parallel on the uphill side of your body and use them to push yourself up (2, 3).

If you're having a hard time getting your skis lined up across the hill, just sit down on your butt and swing both skis around to one side. This maneuver is also handy when you're having trouble making a tough turn. You can always do this and then get up and start again in the new direction.

Traversing

You can also practice *traversing,* or gliding across the hill. Put most of your weight on the downhill ski, keeping the edge pushed into the hill. The uphill ski should be slightly ahead of the other ski. Remember your stance: hips, knees, and ankles flexed and upper body leaning slightly forward. You

should be able to see your hands—they should be at waist level or a little higher. When traversing, also tilt your knees into the hill—this puts more pressure on the edges so you have a controlled and stable ride. The more you push your knees toward the hill the more edge control you'll have. Then relax your knees and let your skis flatten slightly so they can glide across the hill.

Wedge or snowplow

Skiing starts on a flat slope with very little incline. Most instructors will have you practice on the flats, then climb up a few feet to get the feeling of turning. Ideal novice terrain should have a steady, gradual incline ending up flat.

Your first *wedge* or snowplow should start on a flat surface leading to a slight incline. Stand on the flat area, facing down the hill. Put your skis in

Turning. **1**. Keep your upper body quiet and facing down the hill. **2**. Shift your weight to the uphill ski (right ski) by bending your knee and putting pressure on the tip of the ski. **3**. As the ski begins to turn, continue to push your knee forward as you come around and complete the turn. **4**.The original downhill ski will become the uphill ski as you complete the turn.

a V with tips together and facing downhill by sliding the tail of one ski out to the side, then doing the same with the other ski. Balance yourself over this wedge by pushing your knees to the inside and turning your ankles in. Note how the skis tilt up on their inside edges. If you're pressuring the edges, you'll be able to control the skis and brake or glide as you wish. To get coordinated with this move, practice on the flats without facing downhill. On the flats, practice hopping in and out of the wedge with skis together and then apart. Then turn and try to hold the wedge as you move down the hill; release the edges to gain some speed and then increase pressure on the edges to slow down again. Note what's going on: by pushing your right knee to the inside, you're putting pressure on the right ski, causing it to tilt up on edge. Now shift your weight to the other side, putting pressure on your left knee to get your left ski up on edge. While doing this, keep your hands in front with your elbows at a ninety-degree angle.

OK. You've already climbed up the hill, you've traversed across, you've gotten the feel of gliding and sliding. Now it's time to try turning.

Sidestep up the hill a little bit. Start in the traverse position with your left ski as the downhill ski. Push on your right, uphill ski by bending your knee and putting pressure on the front of the ski. The ski will begin to turn—continue to keep pressure on it, working even harder with your knee bend as you go around the turn. As you complete the turn, you'll be back in the traverse position moving across the hill again, but in the opposite direction. Now pressure the other ski and follow the same moves to turn in the other direction.

RIDING THE LIFTS

The chairlift

It's time to ride the chairlift. But there's good news. Most beginner lifts travel very slowly, and the lift attendant will help you get on. Don't be shy: tell him or her it's your first ride up.

Be sure to read the posted instructions. Make sure your jacket is zipped and your ski gloves are on, and get ready to walk through the line or maze at the lift. Start with your skis parallel, and take small, shuffling steps. If there are people behind you,

Tip: Don't look down at your skis: always look ahead so you know where you're going. Feel what your body is doing.

To prepare to get on the chairlift, hold both your poles in the hand that's in the middle of the lift. Look back and be ready to grab the lift as it comes up behind you.

don't move too slowly. If there's a slight incline, jam your poles into the snow and use them to stop you from sliding forward too fast. If you do slide a bit, don't worry—the hill will flatten out. If you bump into someone, it's no big deal. Most other people taking the beginner lift are beginners too.

Take note of where you are in line and be ready when it's your turn to get on. When the person in front of you goes, move up to that spot, and as soon as the lift moves away, step into the loading area. Your skis should be parallel, pointing up the hill. Take off your poles and put them both in your inside hand, the one that will be in the middle of the chair, so your outside hand is free to grab the lift. Turn toward the outside and watch the chair come. Grab the lift and sit down when it touches your thighs. Slide all the way back so you're leaning against the back and keep your skis together. Reach up with your free hand to grab the safety bar and pull it down. (Lifts in the western states may not have bars.) There may be a bar where you can rest your feet. Now relax and enjoy the ride.

The trip on the lift is usually a quick one. Anticipate getting off; look ahead to see where the top lift shack is (there'll be a warning sign before you get there). As you approach the top, lift the safety bar. Move forward a bit so you're closer to the edge of the seat. When you get to the top, put your skis on the ground and use your hand to push yourself away from the lift. Don't use your poles—they might catch in the snow. Try to keep your skis parallel and ski off the lift going straight ahead. Stay on the balls of your feet, and don't look down. Ski forward, wedging to stop.

If you drop something, don't worry—the lift attendant will retrieve it for you. If you fall getting off, move out of the way as quickly as you can. Usually they'll stop the lift.

• •

"**O**ne of the most beautiful things about being on the mountains is going on the lift. The real thrill and what continues to motivate me to ski is the view—the scenery and how absolutely gorgeous it can be even when riding on the chairlift."

—Lisa Winston, owner of Peak Exposure

• •

Surface lifts

Apart from a chairlift, you may encounter rope tows, T-bars, and poma lifts. These are all known as surface lifts because they pull you up the hill, sliding on the snow, as you hold on to them or half sit on them. They are especially popular for beginner hills. With a rope tow you stand next to the rope facing up the hill, with your skis pointed straight ahead and about a foot apart. Be sure to wear your gloves. Get your hands ready by putting the pole straps around your wrists. When you feel comfortable, you can grab the rope with both hands and let it tow you up the hill. Let the rope slide through your hands at first and gradually grip it firmly so it doesn't jerk you. Concentrate on keeping your skis straight and flat on the snow.

A T-bar has bars that look like an upside-down T attached to a moving cable. One person rides on the left side of the T and one on the right. Hold your poles in your outside hand. Position yourself by standing with your skis pointed up the hill. Turn around and watch over your inside shoulder for the T-bar to arrive. As it nears, get ready to grab the vertical shaft in the middle. Don't sit down on the T-bar; let the wooden seat area rest just below your butt so it pushes you up the hill. A poma lift is similar, consisting of a disk on a metal rod that is placed between your legs, but each person rides sep- arately. To get off these surface lifts, let go of the bar or disk and move away toward the slope.

BUYING GEAR

If you've never skied or haven't been skiing for years, renting gear is the smart way to go. In fact, these days even seasoned skiers often rent equip- ment or "demo" (try out demonstrator models). Renting is especially handy

TRAIL MAPS AND TRAIL SIGNS

Winter resorts have trail maps showing all the trails and lifts. Each mountain rates the trails by difficulty using green circles (easy or beginner), blue squares (intermediate), and black diamonds (advanced or expert). A few areas also break down the ratings with double greens, double blues, and double blacks in addition to the single symbols. Double black diamond runs are extremely steep and suitable for expert skiers only. If you forget the trail map, don't worry. There are signs at the start of each trail and at trail junctions naming the run, with the appro- priate symbol to let you know whether it's easy or difficult.

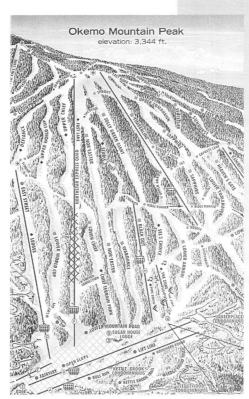

Okemo Mountain Peak
elevation: 3,344 ft.

Trail maps use sym- bols to indicate the difficulty of the trails: green circle (easy), blue square (more difficult), and black diamond (most difficult).

PROFILE OF JEANNIE THOREN: "WE ARE NOT SMALL MEN"

Jeannie Thoren has been preaching to the ski industry and female skiers for twenty-five years about how the anatomical differences between men and women affect the way they ski. For example, she has been recommending that women move bindings forward on their skis from one to three centimeters, because a woman's center of mass is lower in her hips and thighs, causing the bulk of her weight to fall back farther on skis. Moving the bindings gives women a little help in getting forward toward the tips of the skis, which in turn helps us initiate turns more easily. This simple trick was laughed at for years by ski manufacturers, yet now most make women's skis with the binding placement marked one centimeter forward.

Women's wider hips and pelvis also affect the way the thighbone angles in toward the knee, according to Thoren. In some cases this may make a woman knock-kneed, causing her to stay too much on the ski's inside edges. Orthotics in the boots and cants (angled lifts) underneath the bindings can help neutralize this effect.

Another of Jeannie's recommendations was to put heel lifts in ski boots to help women get forward. "I just can't hold myself back when I see a total stranger in pain because of her boots, or struggling because of her skis. About 99.9 percent of the time a simple mechanical fix to her gear makes the problem go away so she can ski off smiling."

Boot manufacturers have addressed some of the considerations of female anatomy. It's standard now to find women's boots equipped with heel lifts. And women's boots have narrower heel pockets and sometimes adjustable cuffs.

There are many other differences between men and women that Jeannie has addressed over the years. She has been instrumental in the development of women's skis, which are now lighter and softer flexing than unisex models, making them easier to turn. In general, women weigh less and have less muscle mass than men. It makes sense to use a ski that is lighter and more flexible.

Jeannie holds clinics across the country addressing all this (see chapter 9, Resources). She travels with a twenty-eight-foot trailer stuffed with more than a hundred pairs of skis, eighty pairs of boots, heel lifts, footbeds, lightweight poles, goggles, and helmets. In her bag of tricks she has everything to lift, shim, stretch, shrink, and essentially tailor the equipment of every one of her female participants. Every woman goes away from the clinic knowing exactly what equipment will minimize her skiing flaws and maximize her potential.

Jeannie Thoren (front, lying down) holds clinics across the country. She helps women pick the right equipment to make skiing easier.

if you're traveling by plane and don't want to lug your gear. You can arrange to demo through a local shop (which will ship the skis to your hotel for you) or a shop at the resort. Many resorts have demo centers with the latest equipment; you can buy a demo pass for the day and stop in to switch models as many times as you like. Many shops do this as well. Even regular rental shops at the resorts now have newer gear. If you rent or demo you can test things like length and ski type while you're deciding whether you like the sport.

Once you've rented a few times, demo a variety of models to narrow down your choices. Even though ski gear can be expensive, there are ways to save. Wait until the end of the season when products are typically marked down, or look for swaps in the off-season at local schools or shops or at winter resorts. But if you can't wait, you may find a good buy even during the season. For example, if you buy a package—with skis, boots, and bindings—you can save substantially over buying the items separately. A medium-priced ski package can range from $450 to $700.

Ski gear changes every year, it seems, but in the past few years it's undergone a metamorphosis. So if you're just starting out or getting back into skiing after a long hiatus, be sure to check out the newer ski designs. The main difference between today's skis and pre-1995 models is in the shape: older skis are straighter, whereas newer

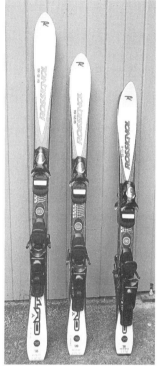

Shaped skis are extra wide at the tip for easier turning.

ones have a more pronounced "sidecut" (the difference in width between the middle and the ends), designed to make turning easier (these new skis are called *super-sidecut, shaped,* or *parabolic* skis).

Women's skis and boots are also much better than when the concept of them was first introduced in the 1980s. Back then a "woman's ski" was a regular model with a pink paint job and a girly name. In the 1990s, though, real design and technological differences were made in ski boots and skis to address women's different physiology and needs. It makes sense to choose gear made specifically for women. Boots are designed with female-specific lasts that have features like narrower heel pockets. Skis are lighter and easier to turn. And you can immediately narrow your choices by steering to the women's gear. Here are some points to note:

- Skis designed for women are generally lighter and softer flexing. This trend continues to be fine-tuned, with some brands now making prototype skis in the lengths that women will use rather than just taking men's skis and shrinking them down, which tends to make the skis stiffer.

- Newer skis may have a super sidecut. Engineers are taking the latest ski designs and adapting them for women. These skis are wider in the tip and tail to make

IF AT FIRST YOU DON'T SUCCEED . . .

The first time I tried a mini-ski, or skiboard (several years ago before they became popular), I was very gung ho, eager to try something new. Off I went to the top of the lift. Then off I went head over heels a couple of times. A few years later I decided to give it another go. Technology had changed and improved. I went out with a large group of ski industry folks—clearly, not the people you dream of demonstrating your tumbling skills to. I was more than a little apprehensive about a repeat performance on these tiny things.

But I liked the feeling of going poleless—it felt so free. I was trying out the Salomon SnowBlades, and they were surprisingly agile. On the flats, I found I could just run in them or skate along to really get some momentum.

My first few turns down the hill went well (I didn't fall), but I felt a bit wobbly. Eventually I found that by working the edges—fully turning and utilizing the SnowBlades sidecut—I could go anywhere at any speed. By the third run there was no stopping me. Soon I tackled tougher terrain. I went through a foot of fresh snow down a double-black graded

Skiboards are mini-skis that are easy to learn to use. Even experienced skiers will enjoy new thrills on the tiny boards.

run, I whizzed down a groomed run at scary speeds—even moguls weren't a big problem on these little toys.

I love to skiboard now. It's a great workout—a real thigh burner if you do more than an hour. It's especially fun if time is short or conditions aren't great.

skiing easier, especially when initiating turns. Several brands have an entire series of shaped skis to accommodate women skiers from beginner to advanced.

- Women's skis have binding mounting points marked farther forward. For years, ski makers argued about whether women needed to be more forward on their skis than men. Now, ironically, most women's skis are marked so the bindings will be installed one centimeter closer to the tips, making it easier to start a turn.

- Women's boots include features that improve the fit for women. Most now have heel lifts to put women in a better skiing position. Several brands also have cuffs that can be adjusted to accommodate a woman's wider calf.

- More women's boots have black as a base color. In general, more aggressive, rich colors with metallic accents are being marketed. No more pretty pastels.

THIS WINTER: GO SHORT AND GO SKIBOARDING!

With all the equipment innovation going on in the world of alpine skiing, *skiboards*, sometimes called *snow skates*, are one of the coolest new things to try. These mini-skis, ranging from 60 to 90 centimeters long, also make it easier for beginners to experience the sensations of skiing. If you already ski, try it anyway: it's fun, it's easy, it's a great workout—and it can improve your skiing.

Perhaps you've seen skiboard competitions on ESPN's X Games, the event where skiboarding made its debut as an official sport.

Skiboards strap onto regular ski boots and can be used for learning to ski, carving turns, skating on the flats, or trying out the snowboarders' halfpipe. The basic moves combine elements of skiing, snowboarding, and skating in one package. Learning is much faster than for other winter sports—it usually takes a couple of days compared with an average of ten days for skiing and snowboarding. Some people who have never tried winter sports pick up skiboarding in a day, especially if they already know how to in-line skate. One reason skiboards are so easy to use is that they're easy to balance and walk on.

Skiboarding is also great if you're bored with your skiing, because the minis can help improve your skills. "If you're not centered, you'll get instant feedback because you'll be tipping over forward or backward," says Sue Spencer, associate executive director of Professional Ski Instructors of America East. According to Spencer, skiboarders can develop a much keener sense of fore and aft balance in addition to lateral balance. It also helps them develop a more active and stronger inside leg movement, which makes it easier to start turning and to actively finish the turn. "That's what good skiing is all about."

Prices for skiboards range from $89 to $299 (with bindings), making them much less expensive than skis or snowboards. And you can pass them around to the rest of your gang for a trial run—skiboards are easy to adjust for different sizes. Most of the major ski manufacturers make skiboards; Salomon popularized the concept with its well-known SnowBlades.

THE EXCITEMENT OF POWDER

"When I figured out powder," says Meg Azzoni, "it was so much fun—that's all I wanted to do. Before I could ski in it, I was always falling. I remember one time in France when the snow was up to my thighs. It was so steep and I just couldn't turn. I was crying because I just couldn't turn." Several powder tries later, Meg figured out the secret for her. "I combined the 'just turn' tip I got from one person with the 'knees together tip' I got from another person, and it clicked. I just did it. It was like heaven —it was so much fun. I was just flying."

Meg Azzoni had a tough time learning to ski in powder, but she persevered. Now she doesn't want to ski anything else. Here she is in the French Alps.

Chapter 7

SNOWBOARDING

One of the fastest-growing winter sports, snow-boarding is like surfing on the snow.

WINTER'S NEW ADVENTURE SPORT

I first tried snowboarding in the late 1980s in a free group lesson meant to introduce ski writers to this new way to slide down the mountain. Snowboarders used one plank instead of two and no poles. Our group was large, and the conditions were icy. We got little personal attention, and I didn't accomplish much in the two-hour lesson. I learned to get into my bindings, and I experienced the quick fall: the board whips out from under you and you land on your butt, hard.

Still, I was determined to learn. But I went about it all wrong. For the first few years I continued to try it about once a year in a free group lesson. Unfortunately, from one year to the next I forgot everything I'd learned. Just because it's free doesn't mean you're getting something for nothing. The best way to learn to snowboard is to devote a few days to learning, or at least a weekend.

As an expert skier, I thought I'd get the hang of snowboarding right away. After all, I knew how to get on and off a chairlift, I knew how to negotiate terrain, and I knew how to sideslip and

• •

"**M**y first day on a snowboard was totally humiliating. I really had a hard time being a beginner, and since I was a well-versed skier, I figured it would be a breeze the first time around. But after I tried it again, it clicked and I loved it. I love the soft boots and I love not having poles. I love the sense of surfing and floating, and the total liberation of the experience."

—Joana Jebsen, 39, Executive Director,
Strategic Publishing Development, Questia Media

• •

edge (pressuring the edges so they grip the snow). All this knowledge can be helpful, but not necessarily in the beginning. Snowboarding is truly a unique winter sport, with entirely different moves from skiing.

You may have heard that snowboarding is easy to learn, with a much faster learning curve than skiing. That depends. I found it difficult at first, but once I got the basics down I improved very quickly. After my years of "free lessons" and floundering around, I finally got serious and decided to devote at least five consecutive days a year to my new sport.

Getting over the hump came during a private lesson. The instructor was great. My problem: I couldn't seem to turn in one direction without falling at the end of the turn. That's because I'd sit back at the finish, putting my weight to the rear of the board and leaving no control on the front half where it should be. I sat back because I was afraid to let go and plunge through the fall line (the straightest route down the hill). The instructor asked if I was a control freak, afraid to let go. That thought helped.

Indeed, snowboarding requires a much more aggressive plunge into the fall line, going directly down the steepest part of the hill as you're making the turn. You have to make a total commitment in every turn; you can't semiturn or use poles to slow you down. Especially in the beginning, it's hard to slow a turn down—it's better to just go for it. Skiing allows much more control in the beginning because you have two skis edging simultaneously to slow you down.

COMMON CONCERNS

• • • • • • • • • • • • • • • • • • •

- **Snowboarding looks so dangerous—will I get hurt?** One way to avoid injury is to start on the beginner hill and not let a friend persuade you to go right to the top! Take a lesson and learn how to snowboard in a controlled manner.

- **Am I too old to learn to snowboard?** It may look like a young person's sport, but more and more "older" people are getting into it. Even people in their seventies have been known to take it up.

- **Is all the rental gear boys' stuff?** It's difficult to find rental equipment just for women—even the boots tend to be unisex. But that's changing as more and more companies produce women-specific gear. In the meantime, just make sure the boots fit snugly and you should be OK. Try renting gear at a snowboard specialty shop where there's a better chance of finding women's demo gear (see gear, pages 109–10).

(continued next page)

COMMON CONCERNS

• • • • • • • • • • • • • • • • • • •

(continued from previous page)
- **Do you have to ski to learn to snow-board?** Not at all. In fact, many surfers and skateboarders take to it immediately without any experience on snow. It is totally different from skiing. On the other hand, skiers excel faster because they know how to slide on snow.

Pick a gentle incline for learning to snowboard.

Brinn Talbot, who loves to try new sports, started skiing at age 4 and learned to snowboard when she was 24. "Something I had to overcome as I got on steeper terrain was the initial fear of pointing the board straight down the hill and just going for it," she recalls. Her latest endeavor: whitewater kayaking.

Even with all my frustrations in the beginning, I loved snowboarding from the start. It felt cool to be hands-free, and I loved the soft boots, which are so much more comfortable than

• •

"I couldn't walk after the first week. Once I start doing something, I know things don't come easy. I'm an athlete, and I know you just have to keep working at it to get it. Sometimes that's the price you pay. It's not only the practice, but the time you spend on the snow to feel comfortable."

—Alicia Klimkiewicz, chiropractor

• •

• •

"It was fun to go back and be a beginner again and progress through something. I found snowboarding a lot easier to learn than skiing—the learning curve was a lot quicker. In the beginning, it's challenging because you fall so much harder. But in three days you get it and can be coming down the hill beautifully. Skiing takes a lot longer to get good at. With snowboarding, you're dealing with only two edges and no poles—it's a lot simpler. The key to learning is to realize that the flats are typically more difficult than the steeps, because it's easier to catch an edge. If you're on a slope, it's just a bit easier."

—Brinn Talbot, 29, public relations specialist

• •

hard plastic ski boots. It was exciting to try something new and to walk around resorts with a board (instead of skis) and have 19-year-olds flirt with me. But it was embarrassing to admit that it had taken me years to master the intermediate slopes when things could have been different.

But today I enjoy snowboarding more than any other new sport. There's so much to look forward to—wide, sweeping carved turns and soft, cushy cuts in fresh powder. They're all new challenges to overcome so I can say "I did it!" Snowboarding is a completely different ride from skiing. The mountain seems more open—as if I could turn anywhere. I love the big, swooping turns my snowboard can make and the ease of plunging through tricky snow.

Snowboarding got its start when Jake Burton (owner of Burton, the world's most popular snowboard brand), started playing around with riding one plank down the hill. He first got the idea from a Snurfer, a sledlike plastic toy that you stand on. From there, he started making snowboards as early as the late 1970s, but the sport didn't really get going until the 1980s and wasn't widely accepted until the early 1990s, when it started to boom. Women have been slow to get into snowboarding, but by the late 1990s numbers were increasing and women were making up close to 40 percent of snowboarders. In the beginning, though, it was definitely a guy's sport, so women who did get involved didn't have much competition and could more easily excel. On the other hand, in the early days it was difficult to find boots that fit or boards designed specifically for women, since manufacturers had no reason to develop them.

GETTING STARTED

The best place to begin is at a resort. Check with the snowboard school to find out about special package prices. I can't stress enough the importance of taking some private lessons. Starting off with a group lesson to learn the basics is fine, but once you get to making turns, a private instructor can really help. For one thing, he or she can ride along beside you, holding your hands to guide you through the turns, so you can get the feeling of turning in a controlled manner.

Group lessons range from $25 to $40, while private lessons can cost anywhere from $50 an hour to over $300 for a full day, depending on whether you choose a small resort or a bigger, more popular spot. As a complete beginner, you can save by signing up for packages that include lift ticket, lesson, and rental gear, which range from $20 to $60.

To save money, go for your lesson midweek, when rates are lower. If you're lucky, you may end up in a class with only one or two others, getting a private or semiprivate lesson at the group rate. And at midweek the slopes are less crowded, so you'll have more room to move around and get adjusted to the hill.

Whereas it's possible to go out on cross-country skis or snowshoes without a lesson, it's really tough to do that on a snowboard. Since it's a high-risk sport to begin with, why take further chances? Before lesson time, though, and in between lessons, there's a lot you can do on your own to help make your first days on a board smoother. Here are some tips on what to expect in the beginning.

RENTING GEAR

Choosing a board: are you goofy?

When you go to rent gear, you'll have to find out what sort of stance you should have. In snowboarding, *stance* means the direction you'll face when standing on the board—you'll either be left foot forward (*regular*) or right foot forward (*goofy*), which is unrelated to your left- or right-handedness.

Every time I was tested for stance, the same method was used. I'd walk into a shop or rental area to get my gear, and the attendant would ask me to stand with both feet solidly planted. Then he'd push me from behind to see what foot I landed on first. And that's how we decided I'm goofy.

Some people feel this method is amateurish. They say you should know which foot is dominant by thinking about how you use your legs. For example, when pushing a car or a piece of furniture, would you push off from your right foot or your left foot? Whichever foot you'd use is your dominant foot, which should be placed at the back of the board to help guide and control your turns.

Anyway, it's more important for some than for others. And if you're technically minded or if you've had any experience skateboarding or surfing, you may notice that things aren't right if your stance is off. Many people I know have switched back and forth time and time again to determine the right stance.

Other decisions you'll have to make when renting snowboard equipment include board size and boot fit. Boards are available in a wide range of lengths and shapes. For beginners, the best choice is a freeriding board that is designed for all-mountain riding (see pages 107–9 for specifics on gear). Choose a board that measures about shoulder height, and try to get one whose width corresponds to the length of your feet. Boots should fit snugly, especially around the heel—you shouldn't be able to lift your heel out of the heel pocket.

Other gear

Choosing snowboarding gear is less of a hassle simply because there isn't as much of it to worry about. And unlike ski gear, the boots are easy to walk in and the board can be carried under one arm.

Some rental shops may rent helmets, although you're more likely to find them at private ski or snowboard shops. Helmet rentals usually run about $10 a day. Other accessories to consider are protective elbow, knee, and butt pads. These are hard to find at rental shops, so you'll have to buy or borrow them. If you in-line skate and have wrist guards, try wearing them over your gloves. Most people don't learn with pads, but it's a good idea if you want to make the investment or are particularly worried about injury. There are also special gloves with built-in wrist guards that cost about $120. Snowboarding gloves are a little different from ski gloves—they're made of more abrasion-resistant material, since you use your hands a lot (to help you get up from falls, for instance).

THE BASICS

Getting into your bindings

There are two types of snowboard bindings: strap-in or buckle bindings and step-in bindings. Step-in bindings were introduced in the late 1990s. They're similar to downhill ski bindings—

you line up your boots at the appropriate spot and click in. The strap-in bindings require more fiddling—you usually have to sit down to adjust the straps, especially if the bindings have highbacks for support. If you're lucky enough to get a step-in binding (which would be rare at a rental shop since they're still relatively new), you can just click into them while standing up—in theory. Some step-ins, however, are easier to step into than others. Make sure the surface is absolutely flat and then you may indeed be able to click in without bending down to stabilize yourself.

Once you're out on the slopes, it's time to put your snowboard on. Before you start, take a good look at the board to figure out which end is the front and which is the back. *Twin tip* boards measure the same front and back, so it can be difficult to tell (see pages 107–9 for specifics on boards). You have to figure it out by looking at the bindings. The front binding has a safety strap (it should be clipped

You have to sit down on the snow to get into **strap-in bindings**. Step-in bindings (not shown here) may be easier to operate.

onto your boot); the back binding doesn't. The front binding tends to be angled toward the front of the board. You can adjust that *stance angle* (the way you stand on the board) as you see fit and as you get better. Also, the *stomp pad,* which is in the middle, where you can rest your free foot when riding the lift, is closer to the back binding.

Once you've determined which foot goes where, you can sit down and put your boots into the bindings. It's best to put the front foot in first. Sometimes, such as when you need to walk or scoot to the lift, you don't put your back foot in at all, leaving it free to help you walk or push along.

Put your boot into the binding and tighten the straps (on strap-ins) so they're snug. The ankle strap (or middle strap if yours has three) should be the tightest, because it's crucial for transferring energy. A snug hold-in over the middle of your foot means better energy transfer, so you'll be able to tip the board on edge faster and easier.

Balance and skating along

In snowboarding, balance is key. And here women get a little help: we have good natural balance because of our lower center of mass. But if you've never skateboarded or surfed you may find it difficult. For me it felt strange to balance on a large surface with both feet locked in.

Practice your balance techniques before you even think about turning. Put your lead foot in the binding and use your other foot to push yourself along. Once you get a little momentum, rest your back foot on the stomp pad and ride along. Bend your knees and drop your center a bit so you're positioned lower—this will feel more stable.

Practice scooting along on your snowboard with only your front foot strapped in. This will help you learn to balance and get you comfortable maneuvering the board.

Practice walking to a specific location (like the lift). Again, the lead foot is strapped in; your free foot walks along and the strapped-in foot slides. It's important to get this down, because when you're in a lift line people will be lining up behind you and you'll feel pressured to move along quickly. You can take your time, but if you know how to walk with your board on you won't feel so flustered. (See pages 106–7 for more on riding the chairlift.) As my friend Joana points out, "It's very bizarre at first when you're trying to walk with a snowboard." Indeed it does feel awkward dragging a big board around, but you can develop a rhythm: first step with your free foot, then slide the board along using your other leg. Just keep repeating to yourself step, slide; step, slide; step, slide. Don't rush it. As you get more efficient, it will feel less awkward and you'll naturally move faster.

Getting up from a fall

It's also useful to practice getting up from a fall. The technique depends on whether you land on your butt or face forward. If you land on your behind, you'll be digging (edging) the *heelside* edge of your board into the snow for stability. (Heelside is the side of the board your heels are positioned on.) Put your hands in back of you to push yourself up, bend your knees and reposition the board so it's flat, with the edge digging in, then walk your hands forward, grab the far side of the board, and lift yourself up to stand. As you rise, keep your knees bent and stay low.

1. To get up from a fall, face the mountain. 2. Bend your knees into the hill with hands facing forward. 3. Squat down on your board with the toeside edge digging into the snow. 4. Get your balance before pushing on the snow to lift yourself up.

If you land face down, rearrange yourself so both knees are facing the hill. Dig the toeside edge of your board into the snow, then put your hands in front of you and push yourself up. You may find this easier than getting up from the heelside of the board.

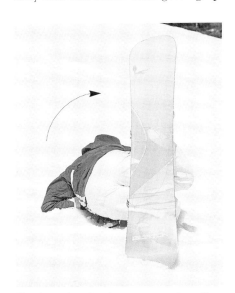

If you're stuck and can't turn, you can always flip over in place to get going the other way. Sit down on the snow facing the bottom of the hill. Lift your board in the air and roll your body over until you're facing the hill with your knees pressing into the snow.

Flipping over: the shoulder roll

Another useful tactic is the shoulder roll, which lets you flip over to your other side. This comes quite naturally. It's useful for heading in the opposite direction when you just can't get yourself to make the turn. Sit down, butt firmly planted in the snow, hands at your sides. Then, lifting your board in the air, roll your body over all the way until you're facing the hill, with knees pressing into the snow. You could practice this without your board in your living room. When you're doing it on snow, just make sure your board is up in the air, leading the turn.

If you really didn't want to turn, you could traverse across the hill (see left), do a shoulder roll, traverse the other way, do another shoulder roll, and so on. You'd never have to turn. That sounds counterproductive and maybe even silly, but what if you end up on a slope that's steeper or icier than you're ready for? With some of these basic skills, you can get yourself out of jams and feel more confident about maneuvering around the entire mountain. Other ways to get across or down the hill without turning are the falling leaf (zigzagging) method and sideslipping (see below for explanations).

Stance

A comfortable, relaxed athletic stance on a snowboard is key. Bend your knees slightly, weight forward. As you're facing down the hill, knees should stay bent, hips should be dropped, and hands should be out front, level with your chest. It's important to be centered on your board, with your weight over your feet. Don't "sit" when lowering your hips or you'll put too much weight toward the back. Likewise, don't bend at the waist or you'll have too much weight toward the front. The idea is to have a relaxed and balanced stance with a quiet upper body.

Edging, sideslipping, and traversing

Once you learn to use the edges on your snowboard you can hang out holding an edge forever, a handy technique on steep slopes. There are two positions for edging: the *toeside* edge, where you face into the hill, and the *heelside* edge, where you face down the mountain.

Edging means putting pressure on the sides of your board so the metal edges do what they're supposed to do—dig in and grip the snow. Edging lets you set the board into the snow so you can stand firmly in place. When you release the edge you can move across the hill on either the toeside or the heelside of your board (*traversing*), or you can *sideslip* down the fall line, which is the straightest (and steepest!) route down the hill (the path a rolling ball would take).

Start your toeside edging by standing on the hill ready to move across horizontally, with your body facing the hill. To engage the metal edge on your snowboard, tilt the board into the slope by pushing forward and down on your toes while shifting your weight forward. Keep your knees bent, which will help you dig your edge into the snow securely. Practice releasing and holding the edge by pushing into the hill, then applying slight pressure back toward your heels to flatten out the board. As you release the edge, slowly turn your head to look across the hill and shift your weight from directly over both feet, leaning slightly in the direction you want to go. You should begin to slowly traverse, or travel across the hill, steering your board in a controlled manner.

To engage the heelside edge, stand with your body facing down the hill, ready to move across horizontally. On this side, just standing with your weight over your heels is often enough to hold the edge, but if not you can dig your heels in by lifting your toes. While standing with pressure on your heels, slowly turn your head to look across the hill, shift your body weight from directly over both feet, and lean slightly in the direction you want to move. At the same time take a bit of pressure off your heel edge, and you should begin traversing.

Sideslipping is moving down the hill instead of across. It requires setting the edge into the hill, then releasing the edge by flattening out the board and applying some pressure the opposite way. Sideslipping, which acts like the wedge in skiing, functions as a braking device to let you control your board.

If you're on your toeside edge (with your body facing the mountain), slowly release the pressure from your toeside edge so the board is flat on the snow, then apply some pressure and weight toward your heels (but not too much) so the board begins to slip down the hill very slowly. This motion is a bit like releasing the accelerator pedal on your car. You can control how fast you go by varying the pressure on your edge. To sideslip on the heelside (with your body facing down the mountain), slowly transfer the edging weight from your heel (which is holding you like a brake), to the toes, tilting the board forward. The motion of your feet in a heelside sideslip is like pushing down on the accelerator. Start your sideslips slowly, giving yourself a chance to get comfortable with increasing speed.

To zigzag across the hill, sometimes called the *falling leaf* method, you combine the traversing and sideslipping skills to get you down the mountain without actually turning. You can traverse one way, then the other way, allowing your board to sideslip a bit as you travel in each direction.

Turning: toeside and heelside

To practice turning, choose a wide, open slope with lots of room to maneuver. Mentally, turning is about getting over the fear of pointing the board straight down the hill. Physically, turning is about weight transfer—shifting your weight from one side of the board to the other. To get onto the toeside of your board for a toeside turn, start in a heelside standing position, facing away from the hill, and roll your weight onto the front of your feet in a clockwise motion (toward the front of the board), moving from the middle of your foot to your big toe. As you do this your knee should move over your foot, gradually shifting the weight to the forward part. The idea is to get the edges to shift from the heelside to the toeside. If you just quickly

Top: To make a **toeside turn**, your weight is toward the front of your board, with your knees pushing forward toward the hill. **Bottom:** To make a **heelside turn**, your weight is toward your heels, with the back edge of your board digging into the snow.

rocked forward from heel to toe, it would happen too quickly and you could fly forward and fall. If you shift your weight gradually by rolling your foot, it also moves your knee and hip forward, which helps lead the turn as well.

For the heelside turn, move the opposite way. Start standing with your toeside edge dug into the snow, body facing toward the mountain. Your weight will be on the front of your feet, so you'll need to roll your feet counterclockwise to shift the weight back to the heels. Remember to keep your upper body quiet, with your hands slightly in front of you, in a centered stance with shoulders, butt, and feet all stacked vertically as you move through your turns. The most common mistake novice snowboarders make is to flail around with their upper body while turning, making them feel unbalanced and usually making them fall.

Instructors have different techniques on how to turn and get the feel of the motion on these basics. All this will be covered in your lessons.

Dealing with flat terrain: the frog and other moves

Because most resorts were built for skiers, snowboarders often have a hard time getting from one place to another. Flat spots between trails are tough, especially for beginners. The idea is to carry your speed and ride straight through. But it's scary to go fast when you're just starting out, and it's easy to catch an edge on the flats and fall. You have to ride an almost flat board, which means staying in your stance, keeping your weight forward, maintaining your balance, and relaxing. The keys to riding the flats are limited motion and staying slightly on one edge.

Sometimes there's so much of a flat runout that you can't carry your speed and you'll have to skate along or try other methods. One maneuver is nicknamed the *frog*, because you squat and move along like a frog (sort of), moving your arms in a double-poling-like motion to push yourself and your board along. It's quite a workout.

A more athletic move is to jump along. You really have to spring upward to get enough oomph to raise the board off the ground and move forward. This technique is usually used by more advanced riders.

Of course you can always unstrap your back foot and push or walk along to get out of the flat area. But sometimes you get tired of strapping in and out of the bindings, so eventually you'll find yourself coming up with other ways to get to the finish line.

RIDING THE LIFTS

Riding the chairlift isn't so bad when you think of the alternatives—taking the rope tow, T-bar, or poma lift. These are all basically surface lifts—some you halfway sit on, some you just hold—that pull you up a hill (see page 91). Although these can be tough enough for beginning skiers, they're really difficult for beginning snowboarders. With the rope tow, for example, you have to hold on to the rope and follow a track straight up the hill. If you don't keep your board flat and straight, you can easily catch an edge and fall. Usually the tracks are defined for skis rather than boards, so there are even more chances to catch an edge.

So try to find a practice hill where there's a chairlift. You already know how to walk to the lift and through the line. You'll ride the chair with only your front foot attached to the board. When you get close to the head of the line, start thinking about your next moves. Watch the people in front of you load and quickly move to the ready position. Usually the operators at beginner lifts are very helpful and will help you load; they may even slow the chair down. When it's your turn, move to the loading area and look over your outside shoulder so you can grab the side support when the chair arrives. If you're on a quad or triple chair lift, try to ride on the outside so you won't have to deal with people on both sides when getting off. Once you're on the chair, pull down the safety bar (if there is one) and use the foot bar (if there

Good snowboarders like to carve, making fast, swooping turns so low their hands almost touch the snow.

is one) to rest your board. If not, you can rest the tail of the board on the toe of your free foot. It's a strain to have the board dangle. After you've settled in, relax and enjoy the ride.

As you approach the top (usually there's a little shack at the end and a warning sign before you arrive), prepare to unload. Lift the safety bar and inch forward in the seat so you're closer to the edge. Make sure the board points straight forward when getting off! Because your back foot is free, you'll place it on the stomp pad so you have two feet on the board for a more stable ride. There may be a slight downhill slope, but it will flatten out. As you get to the unloading area, place your outside hand on the seat and push yourself off smoothly. As you ride off the lift, stay in a low position with your knees bent and your weight slightly forward. Look ahead to where you're going, not down at the board. If you're stuck in the middle on a quad or triple chair, let the others know you're new at this so they can steer clear of you when getting off. Try to go straight ahead after getting off the lift and turn left or right only if you have to. Make sure no one is in your way when you're turning.

If you fall, don't worry! The lift operator will stop the lift so you can get up and get out of the way of traffic.

BUYING GEAR

Snowboards

Snowboards come in many shapes and sizes, and the equipment is changing quickly. There are boards for *freestyle* (short, for doing tricks and catching air), boards for *freeriding* (longer designs for all-mountain cruising and powder turns), and *alpine* boards (strictly for carving turns and going fast). The most popular are the all-mountain, freeriding boards that work well in a variety of terrain—from the *halfpipe* (a snow stucture with built-up walls designed for doing tricks) to the powder.

TRAIL MAPS AND TRAIL SIGNS

• • • • • • • • • • • • • • • • • •

Winter resorts have trail maps showing all the trails and lifts. Each mountain rates the trails by difficulty using green circles (easy or beginner), blue squares (intermediate), and black diamonds (advanced or expert). A few areas also break down the ratings with double greens, double blues, and double blacks in addition to the single symbols. Double black diamond runs are extremely steep and suitable for expert riders only. If you forget the trail map, don't worry. There are signs at the start of each trail and at trail junctions naming the run, with the appropriate symbol to let you know whether it's easy or difficult.

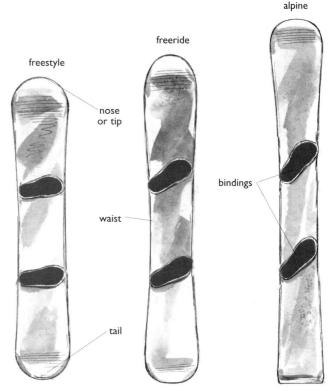

Snowboard anatomy: Nose or tip (front), waist (middle), and tail (back). Nose and tail curve up slightly.

Freestyle boards also are called *twin tips* because they have the same dimensions on both ends and can go backward or forward. They're a good choice if you want to do jumps and tricks or if you do most of your riding in *terrain parks* (special areas with constructed jumps and terrain obstacles for variety and fun). Although freeride boards can be ridden *fakie* (backward), they're designed to go forward.

Freeride boards have distinct tip and tail designs. They're a bit stiffer than freestyle boards, but not as stiff as alpine boards, which are better for advanced riders who have mastered the carve. Alpine boards are used with plate bindings and hard boots. Freestyle and freeride boards are the most versatile, best for those who like to ride all over the mountain.

Lengths can range from 140 to 170 centimeters for women. And what you choose depends on the type of riding you want to do as well as your weight, height, and ability level. Don't buy a board that's too short. It will feel slow and you won't have as much control because of the lack of edge. Get one that's at least as high as your shoulders, but not higher than you. Width is also important. Choose a board that's just about as wide as your feet are long. If your toes hang over the edge, they'll catch on the snow when you turn. And if they're too far back from the edge, you won't have enough leverage to turn well.

If you're just starting, a soft-flexing board is better. Softer flexes twist more easily for smaller, lighter, or less advanced riders. A board with a deeper sidecut is also easier to turn. (*Sidecut* refers to the curve of the board—the difference in width between the middle and the ends. The more side-cut it has, the easier it is to turn.) If you plan to just carve and ride fast, a stiffer board provides stability. Stance angle is important, and instructors recommend a slightly forward-angled stance for beginners. If the stance is not angled enough—if your toes face the side of the board—

Women's boards come in all shapes and sizes and feature lightweight construction with a narrower waist for quicker and easier turning.

you'll have trouble facing your body toward the front of the board and controlling turns. If the angle is too far forward—if your toes point straight toward the front of the board—your hips will be pointed too sharply downhill. The board will react faster to your movements, and it will be hard to control the speed of your turns. Make sure your stance is angled slightly forward.

Height, weight, and type of riding all affect what board you should buy. Try to find a good snowboard shop where an experienced rider can help you decide.

Before you buy

If you've never snowboarded before, renting gear is the smart way to go. In fact, these days even experienced riders often demo (try out demonstrator models) or rent equipment. Rental or demo equipment is especially convenient if you're traveling by plane and don't want to lug your gear. You can arrange to demo through a local shop (which will ship the board to your hotel for you), or a shop at the resort. Many resorts have demo centers with the latest equipment; you can buy a demo pass for the day and stop in to switch models as many times as you like. Many shops offer this option as well. Even regular rental shops at the resorts now have newer gear. If you rent or demo you can test things like length and board type while you're deciding whether you like the sport.

Once you've rented a few times, demo a variety of models to narrow down your choices. Even though a quality performance snowboard setup (board and bindings) can be expensive, usually upward of $400, there are ways to save. Wait until the end of the season when products are typically marked down, or look for swaps in the off-season at local schools or shops or at winter resorts. Check the bulletin boards at supermarkets near the mountain.

Women's gear

Boards meant specifically for female riders feature super-lightweight construction and narrower waists, providing a more efficient energy transfer that translates into quicker and more precise turns. When a board is too wide, it's more difficult to push your feet and get the board to turn; a narrower waist helps get the board up on edge faster. In general women's boards are shorter, although some women's series offer a full range of lengths to suit individuals' riding preferences. Flexes are softer, but board makers have tried to avoid making them too "noodly," so they have some holding power.

Boots and bindings

As with boards, there are different boots for different styles of riding—freestyle, freeride, or alpine. The biggest difference is in the level of support they provide. Freestyle boots are soft and flexible; freeride boots are also "soft" but offer more support; and alpine boots have hard plastic shells to offer maximum control for carving turns. Boots and bindings must be compatible. Boots for women improve every year. It's important to find boots that wrap your feet snugly, holding your heels down but allowing your toes to move. Generally women's boots are lighter and narrower than unisex models. Because they're made on a woman's last, they have a narrower heel pocket, which helps keep the heel from lifting when you turn. Also, cuffs are designed specifically to accommodate a woman's larger calf muscle; they're generally shorter and wider.

Convenience factors have also improved. Look for features that can save you time out on the slopes when you don't want to fuss with boots and bindings—laces that tighten easily or buckle reinforcements for more power and support. Treads on the soles help you walk on the snow more easily or hike up the halfpipe without slipping.

There are two main types of bindings: strap-in and step-in. Many incorporate highbacks in their designs, offering support in the rear. Bindings are now available in smaller sizes to match women's smaller feet. (See page 101 for more on bindings.)

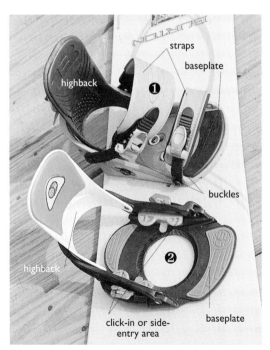

Snowboard binding anatomy: mounted on a single snowboard for illustration purposes are both strap-in (1) and step-in (2) binding types.

Chapter 8

🩰 **ICE-SKATING**

Ice-skating was my first winter sport. I remember flying across a pond with the wind rushing by. Everyone was watching me and marveling at my talents. That's because I was all of three years old! My trick: I was wearing double-bladed skates—a great invention. They should make them for all ages so newbies can get the feel and enjoy the fun without having to balance on a single blade at first.

> "**A** lot of older women . . . are coming into [speed skating] now. . . . Speed skating is a lot more fun than jogging —and it's a lot more exciting."
>
> —Shirley Yates, executive secretary of the Amateur Speed Skating Union of the United States

From then on I skated every winter. If it wasn't cold enough to skate on a lake or pond, my mother, who also enjoyed skating, would take us to indoor rinks. My favorite times were during my teenage years, skating at the local outdoor rink. It would be colder than cold, but that didn't deter the dozens of people who showed up on weeknights. There was always a big fire in the rest area, so you could warm up as you needed to. On the really cold nights I'd smear Vaseline all over my face to block the wind.

Although there's disagreement about when someone first attached a sharp, bladelike device to a shoe for sliding along on ice, established ice-skating competitions for men and women were

COMMON CONCERNS

- **What if I fall backward?** There are ways to avoid falling backward while ice-skating. The most important trick is to keep your weight forward, bending your knees and keeping your hands out in front of you. If you concentrate on doing this, it's almost impossible to fall backward.

- **How will I know if the ice is thick enough?** Ice thickness won't be an issue if you avoid lakes and rivers where the water is deep and dangerous if you fall in. Public rinks usually have a water depth–ice thickness of only a few inches. (See sidebar next page.)

- **What if I can't stop?** It's natural to wonder how you'll stop when you get going on a slippery surface. But once you learn some basics you'll see that you can control your speed and stop when and where you want. There are several ways to stop on ice skates. You can drag a foot or do a wedge stop or a hockey stop (see page 119).

- **What if I have weak ankles?** You probably just think your ankles are weak because they are hard to keep straight in the skates. If you're concerned about this, try a skate with excellent ankle support.

Ice-skating is one of winter's most accessible sports. Where it's cold enough, rinks are often set up by the town each year.

held as early as the late 1800s. And, by 1924 figure skating was an Olympic sport. Skating is one of winter's most accessible sports, and it's one of the cheapest—usually free with a small fee for rentals or lessons. If you live where winters are cold, chances are there's organized outdoor ice-skating right in your town, often at a municipal rink. The town usually monitors the ice conditions, posting some sort of signal (like a flag) that the ice is safe to skate on. Many town rinks are simply a few inches of water on a slightly sunken field. It's also possible to flood your lawn, so you could even skate in your own backyard.

If you don't live where winter thrives, all is not lost. Indoor ice-skating rinks are becoming commonplace in more southern locales and even operate in the summertime. As Geri Gourley says, "Skating in Sun Valley, Idaho, in the summer is nirvana to me. It's the only place in the country where you can skate [outdoors] in the summer. It's so cool to skate outside in your shorts!" Speaking of summer, in-line skating is an excellent off-season training method. It uses all

WHEN ARE YOU SAFE ON ICE?

Although lakes, ponds, and creeks are potential ice-skating spots, I would not recommend skating on them unless you live where temperatures stay below freezing for most of the winter. Ice must be several inches thick before it's safe to skate on. If it looks questionable, don't risk it, and never skate alone in iffy conditions. Rivers and creeks are even trickier because currents can cause moving water to freeze unevenly and weaken the ice.

It's hard to give definite guidelines for what areas are suitable for ice-skating; some places that may have been safe in the past experience environmental changes that affect how the ice freezes. For example, increased vegetation can affect ice thickness. Wind can force water up from underneath, eroding the edges of the ice. Snow over ice can be good or bad. It can insulate ice to keep it strong, but it can also hide cracked and weak ice. Avoid any ice that looks slushy.

Remember that shallow areas freeze faster than deeper spots. It takes a lot of experience to read the ice for safety. Never assume the ice will be thick enough to support your weight. As a general rule, ice should be at least two inches thick for one person and four to six inches thick to support a few people who are spread out on the surface (not all standing in one place). Experts recommend making holes at intervals to check the thickness as you move farther out on the ice. New ice is generally stronger than old ice. River ice is usually about 15 percent weaker than pond or lake ice.

Lakes in parks will generally be patrolled by park officials who will make sure the ice is safe to skate on. With a shallow pond that you know isn't over your head you don't have to worry quite as much about ice thickness, but hypothermia is still a serious danger if you fall in the water.

Despite its potential dangers, natural ice is a great place for skating, especially lakes and ponds that freeze to a nice smooth finish. With a bit of common sense, you can enjoy yourself safely. Obviously, if people are driving cars to their ice-fishing houses in the middle of the lake, chances are the ice is solid.

the same muscles and many of the moves that ice-skating does. If you already know how to in-line skate, you'll pick up ice-skating easily.

IT'S NOT JUST FIGURE SKATING ANYMORE

Skating is an easy sport to learn—in less than an hour you can be gliding along. Most ice-skating is recreational—just skating around and around a rink or pond for the exercise and the pleasure of being outdoors. Eventually you may want more out of the sport, though, and there are several directions to pursue: hockey, figure skating, and speed skating. When you're starting out it doesn't matter whether you use hockey skates or figure skates. Choose whatever is comfortable for you. But if you already know you want to pursue a specific discipline, buy your skates accordingly.

Hockey skating is all about precision and power. You have to be able to turn and stop on a dime at high speeds whether you're going forward or backward. *Figure skating* is more elegant and graceful—those who do it well look like they're dancing on the ice. Although the term "figure" came

IN-LINE SKATING VERSUS ICE-SKATING

In-line skating is a very new sport compared with ice-skating, but its popularity is soaring. There are even classes for learning artistic dance and freestyle maneuvers on in-line skates. There are hockey leagues and speed skating clubs as well.

If you're an in-line skater, ice-skating should be easy for you. Ice-skating isn't as fast, and you won't have hills to worry about. Ice is also a lot smoother than pavement, without those nasty little stones and twigs that can make you fall. You can come to a fast stop on ice skates, whereas on in-line skates you need to slow down gradually. The basic moves of in-line skating (like crossovers) are similar to ice-skating maneuvers.

However, skating on asphalt feels quite different from skating on ice, which is more slippery and harder to grip. It will take some time to adjust. It shouldn't be long, though, before you find the right balance and rhythm. Some people think in-line skates provide more support than ice skates, particularly for keeping your ankles straight. But experienced ice-skaters say that if you buy good-quality, well-fitting leather ice skates they're just as supportive, if not more so.

Figure skating is elegant and graceful.

from making patterns that looked like the number 8, few figure skaters concentrate on this type of skating anymore. Spinning, jumping, and doing gymnastic maneuvers in the air are the ultimate goals of serious figure skaters, and many now refer to their skating as freestyle. This type of skating is far more physical than just skating recreationally. *Speed skating* is also intensely physical, with skaters moving at very high speeds. It's hard to find rinks intended just for speed skating; most people practice at regular rinks and have to travel to specialized training areas. (See chapter 9, Resources, for information on where to go.)

Hockey

Although figure skating is undoubtedly the most popular Olympic winter sport to watch, women's ice hockey is gaining ground, especially since the United States women's Olympic team won the gold medal at the 1998 Nagano games. Tens of thousands of young girls are now participating both in and out

PROFILE OF GERI GOURLEY:
"OK, SO I'M NOT A TEENAGER ANYMORE"

Remember, you don't have to be a teenager to get into serious skating. Geri Gourley, 45, started skating seriously when she was 35. She thought it would be fun to take her 4-year-old son skating. She had skated as a child but hadn't been on the ice in at least fifteen years. "When I got on the ice, I was shocked that I was still able to skate," she recalls. She kept skating and started taking lessons, eventually working with a coach for jumping. "When you learn as an adult, it can take a year to learn something that should take three weeks. Some things came really easily to me, and some things didn't. I would work on a jump over and over again. As they got harder, they got scarier." Geri took lessons for five years, working out four times a week for two to three hours a session. "I had a natural ability to express myself on the ice. I think it was because I did a lot of acting as a teenager—you just learn how to move and express yourself." Even though it took her longer to learn some things than it would have taken a 12-year-old, there were advantages to sticking with it. "I couldn't pinch an inch of fat on my legs," she said. She also did a lot of upper-body weight training to help her "get up in the jumps."

of school. Indeed, more and more women of all ages are joining hockey leagues, both organized and informal.

Contrary to what you might think, women playing ice hockey is not new. Women first played hockey in Canada in the 1890s decked out in long skirts and sweaters. To join a team, call or visit a local rink or hockey organization. Or try contacting hockey organizations on the Internet for information on women's leagues in your area. (Check out chapter 9, Resources, for useful Web sites.)

Speed skating

Speed skating is another variation of exercise on ice, and more and more women are taking it up. "A lot of older women [forties, fifties, sixties] are coming into it now. They were into skating when they were young, and now they're looking for fun ways to stay in condition. Speed skating is a lot

More and more women are joining **ice hockey** leagues.

PROFILE OF LEA SANFORD:
HOW SHE FOUND ICE HOCKEY IN TEXAS

Lea Sanford was never a very athletic person, although she kept in shape a bit by riding horses throughout her childhood. She even had trouble passing her PE class in high school. All that changed in the mid-1990s when she was in her mid-twenties and decided she'd like to try ice hockey after watching games on ESPN. Her thoughts? "This looks like a lot of fun, and I'd be willing to do it just to get in shape."

So off she went to one of Houston's two ice-skating rinks—she was out of shape and had never put on ice skates before. She took six months of hockey skating classes before she started playing, and she got in shape in spite of herself. Her advice? "Ignore protests that you're too old or that women don't play hockey."

Now she plays two or three times a week on a women's team, a men's team, and the Houston Harpies, the team she helped start. As a developmental team, the Harpies strive to provide a safe environment where women can try ice hockey. They welcome newcomers who think they're too old (they have grandmothers playing on the team), women who have never skated, and women who are out of shape. And the Harpies will even provide the gear if you can't afford it.

When Lea started, things were not so easy. There were three women playing hockey in Houston; today there are over a hundred, with five rinks and multiple leagues. "When I first started, my friend and I were just trying to get good enough to play in the men's league—it never really bothered me that there were so few women." The 31-year-old civil engineer says that deciding to play ice hockey was "one of the single most important decisions that made a difference in my life. The camaraderie of a group of female friends is really tremendous. Before that, something was missing. I didn't understand what was missing until I had it."

Playing ice hockey has also led Lea to other sports. "I'm a lot healthier now. I have better general health and fitness and a better diet." Lea thinks that "every woman should play a full contact sport at least once in her life. It's important to learn that even though someone pushes you or hits you, you can still get up. It's important to be in a physical situation you can control."

more fun than jogging—and it's a lot more exciting," says Shirley Yates, executive secretary of the Amateur Speed Skating Union of the United States.

Speed skating is, obviously, all about speed, and it takes strength and power. Who hasn't seen Olympic gold medalist Bonnie Blair demonstrating the intensity of this sport? Speed skating is like track racing; skaters do laps around a large oval rink, going as fast as possible. It gets so intense that they look as if they'd *have* to fall as they swoop around curves at angles so low their bodies almost touch the ice. Joining a local club is the best way to get started in speed skating. Local clubs (there are about eighty in the country) will rent ice time so speed skaters can have the rink to themselves. (For more information on how to get started in speed skating, see chapter 9.)

Joining a local club is the best way to get into **speed skating**, which requires a lot of power. There are even clubs for youngsters.

GETTING STARTED

The best place to begin ice-skating is at a commercial indoor rink where there are people around to help as well as useful aids like walls to hold on to. It doesn't sound very outdoorsy, but there are advantages. For instance, there are rubber surfaces where you can practice balancing on those thin single blades before venturing out on the ice. It's easy to walk around on the rubber and get a feel for the skates. Also, when you step onto the ice you can use the walls to balance yourself. Some indoor rinks even have aluminum walkers for those first uncertain steps.

Commercial rinks also have instructors available for lessons, with classes for both hockey and figure skating. Be sure to ask about workshops in artistic skating if you're looking to get serious about figure skating.

Outdoor rinks might have a cushioned area for practicing balance, but usually you have to get out on the ice right off the bat. You may want to go with an experienced friend who can show you the ropes and be a helping hand—literally.

If your first venture is to be at an outdoor rink, try practicing indoors first on carpeting. Simply walk around trying to keep your ankles straight instead of letting them lean to the inside or the outside. Walking with rubber blade guards on your edges is another way to get comfortable on skates.

WHERE TO GO SPEED SKATING

• • • • • • • • • • • • • • • • • • •

Speed skating is all about going fast. But where can you go fast? Certainly not on a crowded rink. The Amateur Speed Skating Union of the United States can guide you in the right direction. The organization has about eighteen regional associations with links to the country's eighty speed skating clubs. "We're spreading out slowly," says executive secretary Shirley Yates, who notes that there are clubs in the South too. "People tend to think of it as a northern sport, but more and more southern areas are getting into it."

To get started, contact a club in your region. The clubs offer lessons and also reserve ice time at local rinks for weekly practice. The competitive season for speed skating starts in October and runs through April, and competitions are held all over the country. There are races for everyone, from novices to serious professionals.

THE BASICS

Position

When you're standing still on the ice, adopt a position that feels balanced. At rest, you should lean slightly forward with your knees bent while keeping your weight basically centered. When you're in motion, your arms should move in rhythm with your legs, spreading out for balance. It feels somewhat like pushing the air with your hands. It helps to stay low—Hans Brinker-style—for more stability. Hold your head up and always look forward, not down at the ice. Skating is a very graceful sport, and it helps if you act and feel graceful. When in doubt, lean forward. It's when you stand too tall and begin to lean back that you can fall.

Stepping to glide

When you first get on the ice, just stand still until you establish your composure and balance. Then try making some small steps in place. Next, move forward with baby steps to gain a little momentum. Lift your skates off the ice very slightly when starting off. Note how you shift your weight from one side to the other as you walk. Keep your skates side by side and glide forward ever so slowly.

As you glide along, push one foot out to the side, shifting your weight along with it. Keep your arms out to the sides for balance.

Gliding along

When you're gliding forward, push one foot out to the side to gain more speed while the other foot glides along. Push and glide continually, alternating sides rhythmically. As you skate along, shift your weight from one side to the other, using your thigh muscles to propel yourself. Your arms should be out to the sides for balance.

Note the edges on your skates. When you apply pressure to one edge by tilting it toward the inside, the edge will cut into the ice so you can glide along securely.

Practicing balance

Practice going low while keeping your balance. While gliding, bend your knees slowly, ending up in a squat with your arms forward. Maintain your balance while moving forward, keeping your upper body fairly straight and looking ahead.

Getting up from a fall

When you start to fall, try to fall to the side and land on your butt to avoid hand and arm injuries. Don't try to catch yourself with your hands—just go limp. If you can land naturally with a relaxed body, you're less likely to hurt yourself.

To practice getting up from a fall, get down on the ice, leaning sideways on your hip with legs out to the side. Straighten yourself on the ice by getting up on your knees with your hands on each side. Lift one knee and place your skate securely on the ice. Then slowly straighten the other leg as you gently rise, using your hands for balance and to help push yourself up.

Stopping

There are some easy ways to stop or slow yourself down on the ice. The simplest way is to drag a foot by turning the pushing foot outward at a right angle to the gliding foot (forming a T shape) so the edge drags along the ice. Some in-line skaters also stop this way, and it's referred to as a *T stop* in both in-line skating and ice-skating.

The *snowplow* (*wedge*) *stop* in skating uses the same basic moves as the wedge in skiing. As you're gliding forward, bend slightly forward and begin to turn your toes and your blades toward each other, forming a V. Angle your knees and ankles inward to apply pressure to the inside edges of the blades until you slow down and gradually stop.

The *hockey stop* is a little more advanced than the methods above, but it's very effective. Let your skates run parallel, then quickly turn both feet to the same side by pushing on both heels at the same time. This will turn you sideways and bring you to a stop.

To make a **T stop**, (left) drag one foot or turn it outward at a right angle to the other foot. The **hockey stop** (right) offers a fast way to come to a complete stop.

To change directions, cross your foot over in front in the direction you want to go.

Crossovers and changing directions

By learning how to do a *crossover*, you can change directions. Glide forward and get some speed going. Look ahead to the direction you want to turn (in this case left) and cross your right foot over your left as your left foot glides forward (see drawing above, 1); it will come even with your right, but keep it moving forward (2) until your feet are parallel again and uncrossed (3). Bring the right foot over again and repeat the procedure until you've made your turn. When your right foot crosses over, you'll have to lift it off the ice ever so slightly. Also, as you cross over with your right foot, swing your right arm forward in the same direction as your right foot; your left arm stays out to the left side. As you cross over with your right foot, you'll land on the inside edge of your right skate.

Skating backward

To skate backward, look over your shoulder to the direction you want to move. Of course, it's best to practice skating backward when there aren't many people around.

Start with your knees bent and your toes pointing slightly toward each other (1). Push one foot back, then the other (2); as you push one foot back, it should move toward your other heel

Glance over your shoulder as you **skate backward** so you can stay on course and stay clear of obstacles and other skaters.

(3), but before it gets too close, curve it outward and push it backward again (4). As you skate backward, your heels will continue to move toward each other before you start to push backward again with first one foot, then the other. The track should look like the outside part of a figure eight. The tracks your skates leave on the ice are known in skate-speak as a *swizzle*. (See drawings above.)

BUYING GEAR

Choosing skates

Ice-skating doesn't require as much gear as the other winter sports covered in this book. Basically all you need is a pair of skates. Most organized rinks—whether indoors or outdoors—offer skate rentals for as little as $2.50 per session. If you decide to play hockey or take up speed skating, you'll need protective gear as well. For hockey, consider shin guards, a face mask, a helmet, gloves, and protective padding for elbows, shoulders, and butt.

Recreational skating doesn't require expensive skates, but make sure you're investing in a good-quality pair that offer firm support. The most common skates have boots made of molded plastic or nylon-reinforced leather. Prices for used skates generally start at $25, although if you're lucky you might find a pair for $10 at a tag sale. New skates mostly range from $50 to $200. Expert skaters, though, will pay hundreds more just for the boots (shoe part of the skate), which are made of a high-quality, stiff leather that needs breaking in. Custom skates can go as high as $800.

If you decide to buy used skates, look on sports-shop bulletin boards, in consignment shops, or in classified ads. Also, check out pro shops at ice-skating rinks. When buying used skates, beware of any that are too worn—skates with little or no support can let your ankles turn in, leaving you without control. Check to see if used skates need to be sharpened (see page 123).

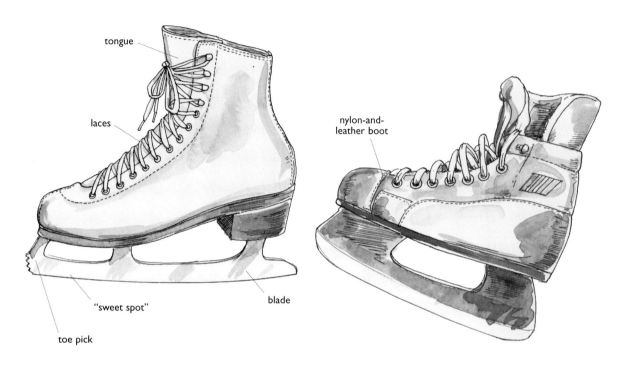

Figure skates (left) are the most common type of skates. The blades have serrated points designed for doing maneuvers. **Hockey skates** (right) have straight blades.

You can skate in either figure skates or hockey skates. Figure skates have blades with ser-rated points (called the toe picks) designed for doing maneuvers. The toe picks also help control speed. Hockey skates have straight blades and offer a more stable ride at high speeds. Women's hockey skates are a new development. There's still a lot more selection in men's skates; women's skates tend to hit the middle of the range, leaving few choices. Speed skates are designed for rac-ing and can be difficult to find and expensive (usually $250 and up). You can recognize speed skates because the blades are very long, extending slightly past the toe and heel. You can learn the basics of speed skating on other skates, but if you're serious you'll need speed skates eventu-ally. The Amateur Speed Skating Union of the United States has information on where to find them. (See chapter 9.)

No matter what skates you buy, make sure they fit. If you're having trouble finding a good fit, consider boys' skates (they're cheaper, too). And because skates vary a lot from brand to brand, you should try on many pairs before purchasing.

Whether you're renting or buying, wear one pair of lightweight synthetic socks (about the weight of tights) that won't bunch up. If you wear tights, make sure they're not cotton, and resist the urge to wear two pairs if it's cold out because that can cut off your circulation or cause chaf-ing. Start with skates that are a size or two smaller than your shoe size. Like running shoes or sneakers, some tend to run wider while others fit more narrowly. Ask the salesperson to tell you what type of feet you have if you don't already know. Someone who is experienced in analyzing feet can give a more accurate assessment.

When evaluating the fit, note that the blades should be straight and centered on the bottoms of the boots. The skates should feel snug, but your toes should not touch the very front of the skates. The heel area should be rigid enough to provide good ankle support—the boot material should not wrinkle up around your ankles. There are heel counters around the ankles to provide support, and you should be able to feel them, but there should also be enough padding to protect you from pressure points and to make the skates comfortable. The toe cap should also be rigid enough to provide protection. If you have to overtighten the laces to get a snug feel, chances are the skates are too big. If you're not sure of the fit, take out the inner linings and see how the skates fit without them (then put them back in). In the end, the skates should be snug without allowing excess movement.

Caring for skates

Caring for your skates properly is important. Wipe the blades after each use to prevent rusting. Blade guards will protect your edges while you're walking off the ice. Have your blades sharpened at least once a season; some skaters (especially hockey skaters) sharpen them after every five or six hours of use. For smooth skating, it's important that the edges be free of nicks and burrs. Some ice surfaces will be rougher on blades than others, so check regularly for signs of dullness and wear. Skating rinks and pro shops have sharpening services. Most serious skaters will have custom sharpening done by specialists who use a combination of hand and machine work. Some skaters carry honing stones to spruce up dull edges. If you've been skating on a dull edge, you'll find it quite a change when you switch to the sharper edges—be careful.

WHAT TO WEAR

Figure skaters might wear either traditional, slightly formal outfits or more practical attire. Many women like to wear a short dress or a skirt and body suit with tights, so their legs are freer to move. But tight-fitting, stretchy fleece pants or running tights also allow freedom of movement and provide a little more warmth. Hats, gloves, fleece tops, light jackets, and long underwear may all be needed depending on the weather. Layering works well for ice-skating; as you warm up, you can remove a layer or two. Skating indoors will almost always be warmer than skating outdoors. (See chapter 3 for more tips on layering.)

BRINGING THE KIDS

Skating with your kids is a great way to get exercise. Kids can skate as early as three years old, though many teachers recommend they start at four or five when their leg muscles are better developed. One trick for helping young children learn to skate is to give them a small chair to push as they move along: the extra balance adds a lot of comfort and confidence. Sometimes

Skating with your kids is a fun way to exercise in winter.

holding a hockey stick with the blade on the ice does the same.

Kids' skates can range from $30 to $200. Buying used skates is ideal because you can change them every year as your child grows out of them. Prices are generally half the retail price. Make sure they're not too big. Look for trade-in programs at shops. You might consider having your child wear a helmet while skating; it's an inexpensive way to be safe on the ice.

Chapter 9

❄ RESOURCES

Women who are interested in winter sports often don't have a clue about how to get started. And it's no wonder. It's difficult to find that information.

In this chapter you'll find out about special programs and instruction weeks just for women. There are listings of manufacturers that can provide specific information on women's gear. The trade associations can help you with everything from what to do at a resort to where you can find equipment demos.

Although not every resource that's worth mentioning is included, this list will get you started in the right direction.

BOOKS

Carbone, Claudia. *Women Ski.* 2nd ed. Boston MA: World Leisure, 1994.

Carlson, Julia. *Snowboarding: A Woman's Guide.* Camden ME: Ragged Mountain Press, 1999.

Gillette, Ned, and John Dostal.

Cross-Country Skiing. 3rd ed. Seattle: Mountaineers, 1988.

Gullion, Laurie. *The Cross-Country Primer.* New York: Lyons & Burford, 1990.

Loring, Maggie. *Skiing: A Woman's Guide.* Camden ME: Ragged Mountain Press, 2000.

Olmsted, Larry. *Snowshoeing: A Trailside Guide.* New York: W. W. Norton, 1997.

Stark, Peter, and Steven M. Krauzer. *Winter Adventure: A Complete Guide to Winter Sports.* New York: W. W. Norton, 1995.

St. John, Allen. *Skiing for Dummies*. Foster City CA: IDG Books Worldwide, 1999.

Tejada-Flores, Lito. *Breakthrough on Skis: How to Get Out of the Intermediate Rut*. 2nd ed. New York: Vintage Books, 1994.

Walter, Claire. *The Complete Idiot's Guide to Skiing*. New York: Alpha Books, 1997.

Walter, Claire. *Skiing on a Budget: Moneywise Tips and Deals on Lift Tickets, Lodging, Equipment, and More*. Cincinnati: Betterway Books, 1996.

MAGAZINES

Backpacker
Rodale Press
33 E. Minor St.
Emmaus PA 18098
610-967-5171
www.bpbasecamp.com

Cross-Country Skier
P.O. Box 83666
Stillwater MN 55083
800-827-0607
www.crosscountryskier.com

Inside Tracks
P.O. Box 420235
Palm Coast FL 32142
800-829-3347

Powder
P.O. Box 1028
Dana Point CA 92629
949-496-5922

Ski and *Skiing*
P.O. Box 55533
Boulder CO 80322
303-448-7600; 800-678-0817;

800-825-5552
www.skinet.com

SkiTrax: North America's Cross Country Skiing Magazine
317 Adelaide W.
Toronto ON M5V 1P9
Canada
416-977-2100

Snowboard Life
353 Airport Rd.
Oceanside CA 92054-1203
760-722-7777; 800-788-7072
www.snowboarding-online.com

Snowboarder
P.O. Box 1028
Dana Point CA 92629
949-496-5922
www.snowboardermag.com

Snowshoer
2233 University Ave. W., Suite 410
St. Paul MN 55114
651-523-0666

Snowboarding
353 Airport Rd.
Oceanside CA 92054-1203
760-722-7777; 800-788-7072
www.snowboarding-online.com

RETAILERS, CATALOGS, MAIL ORDER

L.L. Bean
Freeport ME 04033-0001
800-341-4341
www.llbean.com

Plus Size Skiwear
Greater Salt Lake Clothing Company

P.O. Box 171422
Salt Lake City UT 84117-5100
801-273-8700
www.gslcc.com

REI
P.O. Box 1700
Sumner WA 98352
800-426-4840
www.rei.com

Stefan Kaelin for Women
447 East Cooper Ave.
Aspen CO 81611
970-925-7266; 888-404-7110
www.toski.com/kaelin/women.html
A retail shop specializing in women's gear

Title Nine Sports
5743 Landregan St.
Emeryville CA 94608
800-609-0092
www.title9sports.com

Totally Outdoors: The Outdoor Woman's Outfitter
P.O. Box 452
Morrison CO 80465
800-596-2243
www.totallyoutdoors.com
Information on clothing and gear for outdoor sports; biking, hiking, cross-country skiing, travel.

WomenSport
P.O. Box 1806
Zephyr Cove NV 89448
775-586-0066
A retail shop specializing in women's equipment.

USEFUL WEB SITES

Cross-Country Ski Areas Association, <*www.xcski.org*>. Cross-country skiing information.

Lifetime Online, <*www.lifetimetv. com*>. Information on women in sports, including details on grants, scholarships, and publications and tips on training.

National Ski Areas Association, <*www.nsaa.org*>. Information on mountain resorts.

New England Ski Clubs (Nordic), <*www.ultranet.com/~rhaydock/ clubs.htm*>. Privately maintained list of ski clubs in Maine, Massachusetts, New Hampshire, and Vermont.

OnTheSnow.com, <*www.aminews. com*>. Ski and travel news.

PlaidWorks, <*www.plaidworks. com/hockey*>.

SkiClub Central, <*www.xnet.com/ ~skiclubs/*>. Lists ski clubs by state.

SkiFest, <*www.skifest.org*>. Annual cross-country festival information.

SkiNet.com, <*www.skinet.com*>. News and deals for skiing (*Ski* and *Skiing* magazines' site).

Snowboarding-Online.com, <*www.solsnowboarding.com*>.

Snowlink, <*www.snowlink.com*>. Latest information on women-specific skis, snowboards, snowshoes, and cross-country gear.

Women Outdoors, <*www. womenoutdoors.com*>.

PROGRAMS AND PLACES

Most winter resorts have ski and snowboard camps for women. Check with the specific resort you are interested in to find out how many women's camps are held each year. Resort trade associations will have specific resort information. Women's clinics teach skills, review equipment needs, and offer après ski activities like massages and shopping.

Adventure Guides of Vermont
VOGA
P.O. Box 10
N. Ferrisburgh VT 05473
800-425-TRIP (800-425-8747)
www.adventureguidevt.com

Escape Routes
Pittsfield Inn
P.O. Box 685
Pittsfield VT 05762
802-746-8943
www.pittsfieldinn.com
Inn-to-inn cross-country and snowshoe tours.

Head/Subaru Women's Ski Clinics
12 Kent Way, Suite 201
Byfield MA 01922
800-432-3872; 800-US HEAD 5
   (800-874-3235)
www.headusa.com/womensclinics.
   htm
Supports National Breast Cancer
   Coalition.

Jeannie Thoren's Ski Equipment
   Clinics for Women

2501 Jefferson St.
Duluth MN 55812
218-724-5809
www.jeanniethoren.com
Clinics held throughout the country.

Plus Size Ski Weekend
P.O. Box 171422
Salt Lake City UT 84117-5100
801-273-8700
www.gslcc.com

Ski for Yourself Camps
Christal McDougall
Women's Sports Works
6204 Simmons Dr.
Boulder CO 80303
303-499-0436
www.womenssportsworks
   .com
Women's cross-country programs;
camp series.

Take Your Daughter to the
   Snow Week
Snow Sports Association for
   Women
4261 Piedra Place
Boulder CO 80301
303-545-6882
www.snowlink.com

Teton Women's Telemark
   Weekends
Exciting Escapades
P.O. Box 520374
Salt Lake City UT 84152
801-359-2554
www.excitingescapades.com

Vail Snow Cat Tours
P.O. Box 2033
Avon CO 81620
970-845-5080
www.vailnet.com

Wild Women Snowboard Camps
c/o Oxygen Media
75 9th Ave., 8th Floor
New York NY 10011
877-SHE-RIPS (877-743-7477)
www.wildwomencamps.com

Women Only Snowboard Camps
c/o Katie Bush
P.O. Box 766
Waitsfield VT 05673
800-451-4574
www.snowevents.com

Women's Ski Challenge
c/o Park City Mountain Resort
P.O. Box 39
Park City UT 84060
435-649-8111
www.pcski.com
Olympic champions and U.S. Ski
Team members coach at these
one- to three-day ski clinics held
at Park City Mountain Resort in
Utah.

Women's Week
Telluride Ski and Golf Company
565 Mountain Village Blvd.
Telluride CO 81435
970-728-6900
www.telski.com
Now in its eighteenth year, this
was one of the country's first
women-only ski programs; held
four times a season.

Women's Winter Escapes Program
Deer Valley Resort
P.O. Box 1525
Park City UT 84060
435-645-6522; 800-424-DEER
   (800-424-3337)
www.deervalley.com
Hosted by former U.S. Ski Team
member Heidi Voelker.

ICE-SKATING

Amateur Speed Skating Union
1033 Shady Ln.
Glen Ellyn IL 60137
630-790-3230
www.speedskating.org

Ontario Women's Hockey
   Association
5155 Spectrum Way, Unit 3
Mississauga ON L4W 5A1
Canada
905-282-9980
www.owha.on.ca

U.S.A. Hockey Girls
c/o Karen Lundgren
Women's Section Director
15868 Silver Lake Ln.
Addison MI 49220
517-547-6565

U.S.A. Hockey, Inc.
1775 Bob Johnson Dr.
Colorado Springs CO 80906
719-576-USAH (719-576-8724)
www.usahockey.com/players/girls

U.S. Speed Skating
P.O. Box 450639
Westlake, OH 44145
440-889-0128
www.usspeedskating.org

TRADE ASSOCIATIONS

Listed here are several resort associations that can tell you about
various winter resorts in their
regions. Also listed are industry
trade associations that can provide
information on manufacturers and
general sport activities. Some of
these associations will also have
information on equipment demo

days at various resorts where you
can test women's gear for free.

California

California Ski Industry
   Association
74 New Montgomery St.,
   Suite 750
San Francisco CA 94105
415-543-7036
www.californiasnow.com

Disabled Sports U.S.A.
P.O. Box 9780
Truckee CA 96162
530-581-4161
www.dsusafw.org

Far West Ski Association
27525 Puerta Real, Suite 100
Mission Viejo CA 92691
www.fwsa.org

Ski Lake Tahoe
P.O. Box 10797
South Lake Tahoe CA 96158
800-AT TAHOE (800-288-2463);
   800-588-SNOW
   (800-588-7669)
www.skilaketahoe.com

Southern California Ski Areas
   Association
c/o Mountain High Resort
P.O. Box 3010
Wrightwood CA 92397
760-249-5808
www.mthigh.com

U.S. Recreational Ski Association
1315 Gene Autry Way
Anaheim CA 92805
714-634-1050

U.S.A. Snowboard Association
P.O. Box 3927

Truckee CA 96160
800-404-9213
www.usasa.org

Colorado

Colorado Cross-Country Ski
Association, <*www.
colorado-xc.org*>

Colorado Ski Country U.S.A.
1560 Broadway, Suite 2000
Denver CO 80202
303-837-0793
www.skicolorado.org

National Ski Areas Association
133 S. Van Gordon St.,
    Suite 300
Lakewood CO 80228
303-987-1111
www.nsaa.org

Over the Hill Gang, International
1820 W. Colorado Ave.
Colorado Springs CO 80904
719-389-0022
www.skiersover50.com

Professional Ski Instructors of
    America
133 S. Van Gordon St.,
    Suite 101
Lakewood CO 80228-1706
303-987-9390
www.psia.org
Offers consumer tips on lessons,
rentals, and new trends for skiing
and snowboarding.

Ski U.S.A.
133 S. Van Gordon St.,
    Suite 300
Lakewood CO 80228
303-989-9699
www.travelbase.com/skiusa

Snow Sports Association for
    Women
4261 Piedra Place
Boulder CO 80301
303-545-6882
www.snowlink.com

Connecticut

Connecticut Ski Areas Association
c/o Powder Ridge Ski Area
99 Powder Hill Rd.
Middlefield CT 06455
860-349-3454
www.powderridgect.com

Idaho

Idaho Ski Areas Association
c/o Pebble Creek Ski Area
P.O. Box 370
Inkom ID 83245
208-775-4452
www.pebblecreekskiarea.com

Illinois

National Brotherhood of Skiers
1525 E. 53rd St., Suite 408
Chicago IL 60615
773-955-4100
www.nbs.org

National Ski and Snowboard
    Retailers Association
1601 Feehanville Dr., Suite 300
Mount Prospect IL 60056-6035
847-391-9825
www.nssra.com

Iowa

Iowa Ski Industries Association
c/o Sundown Ski Area
17017 Asbury Rd.
Dubuque IA 52002
319-556-6676
www.sundownmtn.com

Maine

Ski Maine Association
P.O. Box 7566
Portland ME 04112-7566
207-761-3774
www.skimaine.com

Massachusetts

Massachusetts Ski Area
    Association
43 Fairview St.
Dedham MA 02026-3223
781-326-0968

Michigan

Michigan Ski Areas Association
7164 Deer Lake Ct.
Clarkston MI 48346
248-620-4448
www.goskimichigan.com

Minnesota

Midwest Ski Areas Association
1313 Karth Lake Circle
Arden Hills MN 55112
651-638-9658
www.snowplaces.com

Montana

Montana Ski Areas Association
Red Lodge Mountain
P.O. Box 750
Red Lodge MT 59068-0750
406-446-2610
www.redlodgemountain.com

New Hampshire

Cross-Country Ski Areas
    Association
259 Bolton Rd.
Winchester NH 03470
603-239-4341
www.xcski.org

New England Ski Areas Council
P.O. Box 505
Lebanon NH 03766
603-443-8800
www.snocountry.com

Ski New Hampshire
P.O. Box 10
North Woodstock NH 03262
603-745-9396; 800-88 SKI NH
  (800-887-5464)
www.skinh.com

Ski 93 (New Hampshire Resorts)
P.O. Box 517
Lincoln NH 03251
603-745-8101; 800-WE SKI 93
  (800-937-5493)
www.ski93.com

New Jersey

New Jersey Ski Areas Association
P.O. Box 385
Vernon NJ 07462
www.skinj.com

New Mexico

Ski New Mexico, Inc.
1210 Luisa St., Suite 8
Santa Fe NM 87505
505-982-5300
800-755-7669
www.skinewmexico.com

New York

Ski Areas of New York
2144 Currie Rd.
Tully NY 13159
315-696-6550
www.skiareasofny.com
www.skiandrideny.com

Ski the Catskills
c/o Scotch Valley Resort
P.O. Box 339

Stamford NY 12167
607-652-2470
www.scotchvalley.com

Women's Sport Foundation
Eisenhower Park
East Meadow NY 11554
800-227-3988
www.womenssportsfoundation.org

North Carolina

North Carolina Ski Areas
  Association
c/o Beech Mountain
P.O. Box 1118
Banner Elk NC 28604
800-438-2093
www.skibeech.com
www.skinorthcarolina.com

Southeastern Ski Areas
  Association
c/o Cataloochee Ski Area
1080 Ski Lodge Rd.
Maggie Valley NC 28751
800-768-0285
www.southeastski.com

Ohio

Ohio Conference of Ski Area
  Operators
P.O. Box 163
Mansfield OH 44901-0163
419-756-3704

Ohio Division of Travel and
  Tourism
90 N. High St.
Columbus OH 43215
800-BUCKEYE (800-282-5393)
www.ohiotourism.com

Oregon

Oregon Ski Industries Association
P.O. Box 6945

Portland OR 97228-6945
503-768-4299

Pennsylvania

Pennsylvania Ski Area
  Association
5142 State St.
White Haven PA 18661
570-443-0963
www.skipa.com (under construction)

Pocono Mountain Vacation
  Bureau, Inc.
"Skiing the Poconos Mountains"
1004 Main St.
Stroudsburg PA 18360
570-421-5791; 800-POCONOS
  (800-762-6667)
www.poconos.org

Texas

Texas Ski Council,
  <www.texas-ski.org>

Utah

Intermountain Ski Areas
  Association
c/o Deer Valley Resort
P.O. Box 889
Park City UT 84060
435-645-6615

U.S. Ski and Snowboard
  Association
P.O. Box 100
Park City UT 84060
435-649-9090
www.usskiteam.com

Utah Olympic Park
P.O. Box 980337
Park City UT 84098-0337
435-658-4200
www.slc2002.org/sports/
  uwsp_frame.html

Ice skating, ski jumping, luge, and more.

Utah Ski and Snowboard
  Association/Ski Utah
150 W. 500 S.
Salt Lake City UT 84101
801-534-1779; 800-SKI-UTAH
  (800-754-8824)
www.skiutah.com

Vermont

Vermont Ski Areas Association
P.O. Box 368
Montpelier VT 05601
802-223-2439
www.skivermont.com

Virginia

SnowSports Industries America
8377-B Greensboro Dr.
McLean VA 22102
703-556-9020
www.snowlink.com
www.snowsports.org

Virginia Tourism Corp.
901 East Byrd St.
Richmond VA 23219
804-786-2051
www.virginia.org

Washington

Pacific Northwest Ski Areas
  Association
P.O. Box 2325
Seattle WA 98111-2325
206-623-3777
www.skiwashington.com
www.skiindustry.com/psnaa

Washington Ski and Snowboard
  Industries
P.O. Box 2325
Seattle WA 98111-2325

206-623-3777
www.skiwashington.com
www.skiindustry.com/wssi

Washington DC

Travel Industry Association of
  America
1100 New York Ave. N.W.,
  Suite 450
Washington DC 20005-3934
202-408-8422
www.tia.org

Wisconsin

Ski Chicagoland Association
c/o Midwest Marketing, Inc.
P.O. Box 236
Lake Geneva WI 53147
262-723-5633; 800-55 GO SKI
  (800-554-6754)

Wisconsin Ski Industries
  Association
c/o Midwest Marketing
  Organization, Inc.
P.O. Box 236
Lake Geneva WI 53147
262-723-5633; 800-55 GO SKI
  (800-554-6754)
www.skiwi.org

Wyoming

Ski Wyoming, Inc.
c/o Jackson Hole Mountain Resort
P.O. Box 290
Teton Village WY 83025
307-739-2633
www.jacksonhole.com

MANUFACTURERS

Please note that this is not a comprehensive list. Listed here are vendors mentioned in earlier chapters and worthy specialists in women's

products. Also, check with these manufacturers for information on free demo days where you can test women's gear at selected resorts.

686 Enterprises
P.O. Box 1359
Manhattan Beach CA 90267
310-530-9686
www.686enterprises.com
Snowboard apparel.

Alpina Sports
P.O. Box 24
Hanover NH 03755
800-425-7462
www.alpinasports.com
Downhill and cross-country ski boots.

Betty Rides
130 SE 53rd Ave.
Portland OR 97215
503-235-8770
www.bettyrides.com
Outerwear and snowboarding apparel.

Bombshell
25830 Piuma Rd.
Calabasas CA 91302
818-222-0138
Snowboard apparel.

Burton Snowboards
P.O. Box 4449
Burlington VT 05406-4449
800-367-2951
www.burton.com
Snowboards and boots.

Cloudveil
P.O. Box 11810
Jackson WY 83002
307-734-3880; 888-763-5969
www.cloudveil.com
Outerwear.

Cold as Ice, Inc.
234 E. 17th St., Suite 116
Costa Mesa CA 92627
949-642-6790
www.coldasice.com
Snowboard apparel.

Crescent Moon Snowshoe Co.
1199 Crestmoor
Boulder CO 80303
303-494-5506; 800-587-7655
www.crescentmoonsnowshoes.com

Deep
1218 West Yarnell Drive
Larkspur CO 80118
719-481-4513
Snowboard apparel.

Dolomite
19 Technology Drive
West Lebanon NH 03784
800-257-2008
Ski boots.

Elan
P.O. Box 457
Williston VT 05495
800-950-8900
www.elanskis.com
Skis.

Fischer
44 Locke Rd.
Concord NH 03301
800-844-7810
www.skifischer.com
Downhill and cross-country skis.

Head Sports
12 Kent Way, Suite 201
Byfield MA 01922
800-432-3872, 800-US HEAD 5
  (800-874-3235)
www.headusa.com
Skis and boots.

Ibex Outdoor Clothing
P.O. Box 297
Woodstock VT 05091
802-457-9900
www.ibexwear.com

Isis
73 Prim Rd., #309
Colchester VT 05446
802-862-3351
www.isisforwomen.com
Women's outerwear.

K2 Corp.
19215 Vashon Highway S.W.
Vashon Island WA 98070
800-426-1617
www.k2skis.com
www.k2snowboards.com
Skis and snowboards.

Karhu
30 Main St., Suite 430
Burlington VT 05401
888-288-2668
www.karhu.com
Cross-country skis.

Kelty
6235 Lookout Rd.
Boulder CO 80301
800-423-2320
www.kelty.com
Backpacks for carrying babies.

Lange
c/o Skis Dynastar, Inc.
P.O. Box 25
Colchester VT 05446-0025
800-992-3962
www.dynastar.com
Ski boots.

Lowe Alpine
P.O. Box 1449
Broomfield CO 80038

303-465-3706
www.lowealpine.com
Outerwear.

Madden Mountaineering
2400 Central Ave.
Boulder CO 80301
303-442-5828
www.maddenusa.com
Backpacks for carrying babies, skis.

Marmot
2321 Circadian Way
Santa Rosa CA 95407
888-627-6680
www.marmot.com
Outerwear.

Morrow Snowboards
19215 Vachon Highway S.W.
Vachon Island WA 98070
800-272-6215
www.morrowsnowboards.com
Snowboards.

Nordica
Benetton Sportsystem U.S.A.
One Sportsystem Plaza
Bordentown NJ 08505
800-892-2668
www.nordicaboots.com
Ski boots.

Obermeyer
115 AABC
Aspen, CO 81611
800-525-4203
www.obermeyer.com

Olin Skis
K2 Corp.
19215 Vashon Highway S.W.
Vashon Island WA 98070
800-522-7547
www.olinskis.com
Skis.

Raichle
Geneva Rd.
Brewster NY 10509
800-431-2204
www.raichle.com
Ski boots.

Redfeather Design, Inc.
4705-A Oakland St.
Denver CO 80239-2837
www.redfeather.com
Snowshoes.

Rossignol
P.O. Box 298
Williston VT 05495
800-437-6771
www.rossignol.com
Alpine and cross-country skis and
boots; snowboards.

Salomon
9605 S.W. Nimbus Ave.
Beaverton OR 97008
800-225-6850
www.salomonsports.com
Downhill and cross-country boots,
skis, snowboards.

Sierra Designs
1255 Powell St.
Emeryville CA 94608
510-450-9555
www.sierradesigns.com
Outerwear.

Skis Dynastar, Inc.
P.O. Box 25
Colchester VT 05446-0025
800-992-3962
www.dynastar.com
Downhill and telemark skis.

Tecnica
19 Technology Dr.

West Lebanon NH 03784
800-258-3897
www.tecnicausa.com
Ski boots.

Tough Traveler
1012 State St.
Schenectady NY 12307
518-377-8526
Backpacks for carrying babies.

Tubbs Snowshoe Co.
52 River Rd.
Stowe VT 05672
800-882-2748
www.tubbssnowshoes.com
Snowshoes.

Volkl
19 Technology Dr.
West Lebanon NH 03784
800-264-4579
www.volkl.com
Skis.

Yuba Shoes
Pride Industries
10030 Foothills Blvd.
Roseville CA 95747
800-598-9822
www.yubashoes.com
Snowshoes.

CLUBS

70+ Ski Club
1633 Albany St.
Schenectady NY 12304
rtl70+@aol.com

Atlanta Ski Club
6255 Barfield Rd., Suite 206
Atlanta GA 30328
404-255-4800
www.AtlantaSkiClub.org

Boston Ski and Sports Club
70 Birmingham Parkway
Brighton MA 02215
617-789-4070
Fax: 617-254-1990
www.bssc.com

Ski Club of Washington D.C.
5309 Lee Highway
Arlington VA 22207
703-536-8273

Northwest Ski Club Council
   (NWSCC)
P.O. Box 1915
Portland OR 97207
503-243-1332
www.nwskiers.org

Index ❄